RUPERT JONES

The Memoirs of a Motorsporting Clergyman

First Published by Richard Netherwood Limited

ISBN 1 872955 03 7

Typeset in Garamond by 'Word-Up', Huddersfield
Book Design by Richard Netherwood
Cover Design by 'Word-Up', Huddersfield
Cover Photography by Simon Morley, Stocksmoor
Printed by B L & U Printing Limited, Wellingborough

Dedication

I dedicate this book to my wife Sue, who has not only inspired me for twenty five wonderful years but has also put up with me working on this manuscript for the last six months, and also to John and Richard Netherwood, who came to me when I was ill and said "do it". So I have.

Acknowledgements

I acknowledge with grateful thanks that I have used for some detail "Seven Year Twitch" by Marcus Chambers and also "The BMC/BL Competitions Department" by Bill Price.

Foulis. Haynes.

Introduction

I have often been asked "How do you mix religion and motorcar rallying?" Sometimes the question is genuine, sometimes for the sake of something to say, but I find it a difficult one to answer. How for instance do I mix religion with shooting deer or drinking beer or ski-ing or playing skittles in a pub in Somerset? I have never had to pour in any special additive to achieve what to me was not a mix but a natural progression. Fortunate in family, gifted and guided by God and very good friends and teachers, life has gone joyfully from strength to strength, affording me and I hope others, a lot of fun. I hope also that along the way I have been of some help and use to my fellows. So to try to answer the question I have written this book in an endeavour to show, primarily from the side of motorsport and fun and games, good humour and good friends, how there is really no great problem in living close to Castrol R and the oil of Holy Unction, and I write that last sentence in all sincerity. I hope that the book will bring a laughing look at my early motorsport and show the link in my life between rallying and religion.

Foreword — Marcus Chambers

It was a long time ago that I wrote the character sketches of some of the drivers, navigators and mechanics with whom I had had the honour to be associated at a particularly exciting time in the history of International Rallying.

On re-reading what I wrote about Rupert, I feel that it would be hard to do better than repeat what I wrote then.

"Rev. Rupert Jones. His first contact with BMC was with the Cambridge University team which took the seven-day endurance records with the Austin A35 in 1957. Rupert, even then, had made up his mind that he was going to be a priest but intended to go on participating in motor sport as long as he was able to do so. He has shown great aptitude in his chosen sport and is now the Curate of Hamer, near Rochdale. Short and dark, Rupert is a great sportsman with a fine sense of humour. Universally known as 'the Bishop' by the rally world, he is admired and respected by drivers and mechanics alike. A word from the 'Bishop' often makes us remember that Christianity is with us all the time, whatever we may be attempting or wherever we are. Ann Wisdom once told me that Rupert took the team to church in Oslo before the start of the Monte Carlo Rally and someone spoke of praying to win, the 'Bishop' said 'No, you must pray that you will be worthy of winning!' Rupert likes sailing and deerstalking and is, I am told, the idol of the younger members of his parish".

Since I left the scene of Ruperts' activities he has continued his love of motor sport in all its forms with success and has at the same time remained true to his own vocation in that he not only runs a Parish with the help of his charming wife, Sue, but also teaches Divinity in a Yorkshire school. Truly a man of many parts who has now added to his accomplishments by putting his experiences down on paper for us to share them.

Contents

Trials and Army and Austrian Tribulations

The whine of the supercharger somewhere down by my right knee was reassuring. Father pumped the throttle and let in the clutch, the rear wheels fought for grip and we came round the right hander to see the incredible steepness of Simms Hill, a gradient of 1 in 4 and a rock step three quarters way up.

We had failed at the step last year, but with the blower on.... The motorcycle trials tyres on the rear wheels began to grip and we were really motoring when we hit the step, a terrible clang from the girder type front forks and the whole front end seemed to take off, while

"ballast would have won, only it is not very satisfactory to shout and swear at...."
The single cylinder 633 cc sidecar wheel drive Norton.

the rear wheels fought their way over the step and we made it to the "Observed Section Ends" sign. This was the 1954 Exeter Trial and we had already cleaned Fingle Bridge, a well known and delightfully twisty hill.

Before the second world war my father had ridden works Nortons in Trials and in the Manx Grand Prix on occasions along with my mother's brother, my uncle Jim. Mother regularly and successfully competed in Trials with her 1935 Morris Eight. During the hostilities father lost a leg, which made supporting a solo bike somewhat problematic. Taking to a sidecar meant that he required either ballast or a passenger. I think ballast would have won, only it is not very satisfactory to shout and swear at when things go wrong, and as I was the only human about who seemed prepared to set out, that was decided upon. As I was only about ten and a half years old and didn't reach the necessary minimum weight we still had to carry some ballast.

We went to Nortons in Birmingham by train and at the factory Daddy was given a great welcome. We collected a 633cc single cylinder Norton with sidecar and sidecar wheel drive, designed and built for military purposes. The sidecar wheel drive was engaged by means of a lever near the back wheel which operated a dog clutch. Once engaged, left hand corners were virtually impossible and many is the hedge we extracted the device from, after leaving the end of a section with the thing still engaged. It was rather a large and wide machine for some sections, but in those days many trials were for bikes and cars. In spite of size and weight, performance on steep hills was impressive and it really seemed as though it would go up the side of a house. I remember our "cleaning" one steep pitch in North Wales which had never been cleaned by a chair before, and we returned later in the day to see an H.R.G. (Hurg) and a well driven Allard fail within a few feet of the top.

It was during this period of my life that I learned, either because of, or in spite of, much shouting and cursing and swearing, to read, with some accuracy, maps Ordnance Survey. This was to stand me in very good stead in later years.

After local events came the M.C.C. (no, not that innocuous little cricket club, The Motor Cycle Club) events, primarily the Exeter and Lands End Trials, the others were interfered with by education.

Kenilworth was our normal starting point and I suppose that by now I was about fourteen. We usually travelled down in daylight, went to the pictures and then to a pub for sandwiches and HALF A PINT OF BEER. Then off into the night. Those who have never been involved with motor sport fondly imagine that it is all very exciting. Not so, it is frequently long stretches of total boredom knotted together with short spells of high drama, and this perhaps was more true of M.C.C. Trials than many other events.

''sidecar wheel drive... engaged by a dog clutch... 'cleaning' one steep pitch never cleaned by a chair before''
Swan Song hill, North Wales. Jeans Gold Cup Trial 1946.

When we left Kenilworth the first ''hill'' or ''observed section'', although tackled by bikes in the dark, the cars coming through later, was probably some six hours of main road away, with only a stop at a transport cafe after Bristol to lighten the darkness. I liked it when we were a late number in the bike section, because one frequently had time, before ''sections'', to walk back and see the Hurgs and chain gang Frashes, the Allards, Trojans and Dellows queuing up to take their turn.

After the Norton came a Reliant Bread Van off which the top was unceremoniously cut. A hood was provided over the two seats, between which the Austin seven engine was housed, and the pick up truck back end, invaluable for family camping holidays, gained a neat and functional tonneau cover. Because this strange three wheeled device qualified, as did three wheeled Morgans and BSA's, for the sidecar class, motorcycle trials tyres were permitted. The result was that we frequently had more grip than power, causing the front wheel, in the words of the regulations regarding lack of success, ''to fail to revolve in the direction of the set course''. A Shorrocks supercharger was fitted, only tweaked up to four pounds boost, but it revolutionised the ''Hovis Special'' which now had quite dramatic acceleration, a reasonable top speed, and, contrary to popular belief, quite good handling. Well, she would drift on tarmac, if you kept the heat turned well up.

Reliants became interested and Hovis became a test bed for many of the parts to be used on the first version of the three wheeled

"A Reliant Bread Van... with Shorrocks supercharger... cleaning Simms" Here seen on Fingle Bridge.

vehicle car, which Father was persuaded to have one of the first few off the line. Hovis was retired, but not before cleaning Simms Hill.

By now I had my own bike, school was coming to an end and National Service beckoned. Unlike some of my compatriots I looked forward to this challenge. In those high and far off days I was fit, captain of school rifle shooting and boxing, a player of squash, cross country runner, whipper-in for two beagle packs, one during term time, another in the holidays, and reasonably competent on skis and ice skates. I could swim and handle a boat in a rough sea and fish from it as well, but sails were and are still a complete mystery to me. I had done a lot of fell walking and a little climbing. The Royal Marines accepted my application and in February 1954 I went to Lympstone in Devon to be basically trained. It is perhaps worth mentioning at this point that by the time I was fourteen I had decided that I wished to be a Church of England clergyman, after an "experience" in my prep school chapel. I regarded this as quite a normal thing to want to do, I served at the altar and regularly attended services on weekdays as well as Sundays, but from an early stage I decided that it was more important to take my faith with me on my various sporting ventures, rather than to sit at home regretting that I had not gone on the the Exeter Trial.

Basic training was fierce but I enjoyed it, leading the fastest team ever over the assault course as it then was, and being best shot in 849 squad. Some of the lads from Liverpool and Glasgow were suspicious of me to start with but we grew to respect each other and with some I made great friends. There are a few memorable incidents. Our platoon sergeant was one McCluskey. Thus he addressed his charges: "Some say 'you play ball my way, I play ball your way'. I say you play ball my way or its left, right, left, right, clang bang, mind those f.....g fingers ". He made us work but he was full of bull and his leg could be pulled on occasion. Colour Sergeant Sowdon was our drill instructor. A perfectionist, a stickler for discipline but a really kind West Country gentleman. I never heard him raise his voice any higher than essential. He would approach the parade ground from behind us and wait for others to cease giving commands, then, hardly above a whisper he commanded "849 Squad shun". We really worked for him and admired him.

Shortly before we finished our sixteen weeks basic we were herded into a three ton truck just before our evening meal and on the day before pay day. As we closed on Dartmoor the lorry stopped several times and people were abandoned in two's and three's some little distance apart, having been given a map or compass and some whispered instructions by the good Captain Maitland, our platoon officer. I was in the last three as we jumped out when the lorry came to rest again. Maitland arrived from the cab end "Terribly sorry you chaps, run out of maps, only a compass left, can't allow you to set off to meet us in Princetown for breakfast without a map. Have to do the exercise with the next group". Up steps Jones, saluting respectful like, and in his very best officer accent replies "Absolutely no problem, sir, just let me have the compass and any further instructions sir, and we will see you in Princetown at 7.30 am sir". I am being kicked about the ankles with some vigour by my mates. "Well I shouldn't really Jones, but if you are quite sure....?" The lorry turned and headed back to barracks.

When I had quite calmed my rioting troops we managed to raise between us four proper pennies, walk two hundred yards to a phone box and ring my uncle at his farm some three miles away. Uncle Bill had fought in North Africa and Italy and having been assured that we were on an initiative test quickly came to our rescue. We helped about the farm, Aunty Nan prepared a huge meal, and there was adequate scrumpy to drink. An early start and milking was done in record time; washed, shaved and breakfasted, Uncle Bill drove us to a point just short of Princetown, and giving us £1 and twenty

Capstan Full Strength left us to march smartly down the road to the rendezvous. Captains, Corporals and colleagues were aghast. The daylight part of the exercise was completed by bus in time to take a leisurely luncheon of beer and cheese before reporting to the finish. Initiative? Well, good use of local knowledge.

I then went to officer cadet school at Eaton Hall, Chester, very near my parents home, for a much less demanding sixteen weeks, although some of the smoothy types didn't think so, but then some of them didn't pass.

After commissioning I was seconded to an infantry regiment, by chance, Uncle Bill's old unit, where there were several officers who had fought with him in Italy. The commanding officer was not one of them. Lt. Colonel John Willie Staires was an excellent officer but lacked a little humour. I was called for interview shortly after joining the Battalion in Trieste. Why had I joined the Marines? Because, I said, I did not wish to waste my time as some of my friends had done in the Army. I got a very cold look and was told that if I ever found my time was being wasted I was to report at once to him. As I went out through the Adjutant's office the Captain did not speak but shook his head in a way which seemed to say, who was this young national service officer who dared to address John Willie thus?

We spent a few weeks variously on border guard, spraying rioting Italians with fire hoses and raising false alarms when the Americans were on night duty, just so that we could watch them dash about Trieste in their armoured jeeps. Then we hauled down the Union flag and came home to Barnard Castle. Here nothing happened except shovelling coal, then snow, and regular drinking contests against the Sergeants Mess in most of all of that excellent town's twenty seven hospitable hostelries. I applied to see the C.O. and having explained to the Adjutant the nature and purpose of my mission the man looked very sad for me. However I was shown in and explained that I had nothing to do that could not be done in the first hour after parade each morning, and I reminded J.W.S. of his comments in Trieste. A struck match would have set light to the silence. I began to think that I might have made an error of judgement. Then Lt. Colonel Staires spoke. He understood, he said that I thought that I knew something about wine, and he had observed that I liked to eat well, the Mess Officer was going on secondment, I would take over as Mess officer and make sure that there was always an adequate supply of his particular sherry. I should also look around for something to do and then come and tell him.

I was indeed, and still am, interested in food and wine so I really enjoyed that new assignment. I went back to the Colonel in two weeks time and announced that I had discovered six brand new and unused motorcycles, twelve similar rifles and two good as new Bren guns. I wished to form a battalion motorcycle team and to com-

pete in Trials and a shooting team from my own platoon to win a trophy called the Hopton Cup. He thought for a few moments and enquired about the cost of the motorcycle venture. I had my figures ready and that was arranged. The Hopton Cup was a competition for five rifle men and a Bren gunner and in fact there were two cups, one for units serving abroad, the other for those in the United Kingdom. Before my time, the battalion had done well in the overseas section, but at home the trophy had been taken for years by the Rifle Brigade, whose team normally took the first four or five places. J.W.S. thought this might be beyond us, but would not stand in my way. He turned to the somewhat amazed adjutant and said that I was to be afforded every reasonable facility and any problems should be referred straight to him.

"a battalion motorcycle team to compete in Trials" Corporal John Lonsdale, Captain Jack Yates 2nd Lt. Rupert Jones and three of the 16H Nortons at Barnard Castle.

The bikes were 16H Nortons with girder forks, not the nice light 350 cc Matchlesses with tele front forks issued to signals units. They were totally unsuitable even for army events, so I decided to do the Exeter and the Lands End in 1955. Two days before the Exeter I had a very nasty coming together with a lorry returning from leave on my new brand new 197 cc trials James. Father rescued me from the nearby police station on whose front steps I had landed, the lorry driver was warned that he would probably be charged, and, after a beer and a sandwich, I entrained for Barnard Castle. I stood

"...and a shooting team from my own platoon to win the Hopton Cup" complete with Hopton cup and Regimental Sergeant Major Matterson centre rear.

for the journey, not for lack of seats but because I was too bruised to sit. I spent two nights trying to sleep half sitting, half standing and then Captain Yates, Corporal Lonsdale and I set out for Kenilworth. I was unable to start my machine but once it was going I could ride it. All three of us finished but no medals were won. I managed to clean several sections but came a fearful cropper on the aforementioned Simms step. When the 16H and I were lugged to the top I was unable to make an unbelievable dense marshal understand that someone would have to start the device for me before I could take it away. Fortunately, the excellent young man on the tractor who towed up failed cars realised my predicament and kicked her over for me. We felt we had done well to finish and were then faced with an unbelievably snowy, then icy, trek north. We made my parents home in Cheshire on day one and then slithered and slipped to Barney. We all fell off at least three times en route. I was now one large bruise and lay low for a few days.

The Lands End enjoyed superb spring weather and we had a really pleasant run, but still failed to win any medals. Meanwhile I had stripped and rebuilt the rifles and thoroughly tested them. Not having sufficient "know how" to do the job myself I sent the Bren guns to an armourer for a good check up. I found four good shots in my platoon and a national service corporal who was quite exceptional with the Bren. One shot for the Cup on one's own range with a "neutral" judge present who submitted the score to the Army Rifle Association. Derek Duddle had to fire first with the Bren from 300 yards before we all ran forwards and all fired from 200 yards, the whole event being against the clock. Although we couldn't tell his exact score, we all knew before we ran forward that Derek had shot brilliantly. As team captain I not only had to fire my own target

"but came a fearful cropper on the aforementioned Simms step"
a) before b) after

but also had to direct the others, and I had to call to one lad that he was going low, which he corrected, but the others went well.

When the judge gave us our score we were really bowled over, it was five points more than the record. We had to wait some weeks for the results. I was called to John Willie's office to be told the news that we had not only won but by six points, and that the Rifle Brigade filled the next five places. The C.O. was highly delighted and National Service for me drew to a delightful close.

The were some eight months to fill in before proceeding to Cambridge and my uncle promised me some sort of gainful but suitably flexible employment at the factory of which he was managing director in Wallasey. Flexible in that I wished some time for Trials riding, stalking and other important ventures with which work should not be allowed to interfere.

However, before this started my mother felt that the food with which Her Gracious Majesty had so generously supplied me over the last few years would have been woefully inadequate, totally lacking in greens, vitamins, iron and all the other lead free things the human body is supposed to require, and therefore two weeks skiing in Austria were called for. It had to be Austria, for her father, my grandfather, had been an Austrian and the whole country abounds in assorted second, third and fourth cousins. Although we did manage some excellent skiing, it was a holiday fraught with high drama, which is the only reason that makes it worthy of record.

It was a bitter cold morning, coldest on record according to the radio, as father and I folded away the soft top on my mother's Ford Consul, so that our skis could be accommodated. On the fifty mile journey from our home in the Wirral to Ringway we counted thirty eight cars which had boiled to a standstill, while I froze in the back of the Consul. We said goodbye to daddy and were soon on the plane. Derbyshire on the left, Wales on the right as I pointed out to mother, then suddenly Wales and Derbyshire changed places and the pilot announced a return to Ringway due to mechanical failure. We were met by a full complement of fire engines and ambulances, all clearly visible from the air as we approached. We were then put on a flight from Dublin to Birmingham and Paris, diverted to collect us. At Birmingham we showed our passports and went through customs, repeating the process before being allowed to proceed to Paris, which was still not our expected destination. There is not much skiing there. In Paris, customs and passports again, and apart from our little group a new set of colleagues who were under the impression that they were going to London. They were not amused when, after take off, it was announced that they would be going to London but via Zurich. We were accommodated in a good hotel at the airline's expense as it was too late to proceed the hundred or so miles by train to Austria. Once at our resort the bitter cold wind continued and the high lifts in the area were regularly closed because of the cold. This was a pity as neither mother or I are "piste" enthusiasts but prefer what used to be called "touring". Take a high lift, climb on for another hour, perhaps seeing some chamois, ski, in virgin snow, to some other village, take luncheon and then either go up high again and ski back to base by a new route, or if defeated by luncheon return by "Post Bus".

"Mother and I prefer... touring"
Above Zurs, Austrian Vorarlberg.

After a couple of days I developed stomach pains. There had been heavy snowfalls and the pass out of the village was closed. The doctor diagnosed appendicitis and said that if it didn't settle down he would operate, if necessary, using the kitchen table as a base. After twenty four hours on water and absorbing this little threat I made a remarkable recovery. A few days later the biggest and best hotel in the village caught fire, the blaze starting in the attic. Many people set to, to start emptying the place floor by floor, stopping at the bar in the cellar for refreshment between trips. Because it was so cold water was scarce. After an hour the Fire Brigade from Bludenz arrived, but were unable to unfreeze the hydrants. Little fires were lit from the stream to the hotel and the pipes laid over them, but only a pathetic little dribble of water appeared at the operational end. Meanwhile the fire grew apace and the metal roof of the hotel glowed orange in the night sky. After some five or six hours an engine from Innsbruck arrived with foam. In half an hour the foam was exhausted but the fire was not. One wing of the hotel could be saved but the main section was abandoned once the bar was finally drunk dry. In all the fire burned for some twenty three hours.

The cold relented in our second week and we had some excellent skiing. One trip ended in an extended luncheon at Lech. The Post Bus arrived too soon, or we finished too late. Our guide spoke with driver and everyone got off the bus and came into the Post Hotel. Mother bought drinks all round and half an hour later we embussed for Zürs, our resort, and the bus continued on to Stuben and Langen, where it should have connected with a train. I often wondered if it did. In time we set out for home and at Zurich airport observed a rival airways flight set off direct for Manchester with only four passengers aboard, just as the Tannoy announced that our airline would fly their ''Manchester direct'' passengers to London first due to shortage of aircraft.

We landed in London through an appalling thunderstorm which threw our aircraft all over the place. After formalities we were quickly put in another plane for Manchester. During the inevitable revving on the runway I noticed rather more flame than usual from one engine. Sure enough we trundled back to base with the pilot explaining that there were mechanical problems. It would be at least an hour and a half before we could proceed, during which time we would be given dinner. I managed to telphone to father at Ringway, who had been told nothing of our delay. Dinner was much enlivened by a perfectly splendid collision between a waiter carrying twenty four Coupes Jaques and a waitress armed with two large bowls of fresh fruit salad. Both parties bit the dust, scattering their wares in ''toutes directions''. All very colourful and an act not often bettered in pantomime. We eventually made it back to Ringway.

My appendix was removed lest it offend again at some inconvenient hour, and after a while I started work in Uncle's office as a filing clerk. I was not very good at it and got rather bored, although I met some good folk, especially on the factory floor whence I was sent on various errands. I competed in Trials on my James but without success, and as Cambridge approached decided to change it for an early Norton Dominator which could be used either solo or with ''chair''. Solo it made a delightful road bike and with chair was sporting and also carried luggage. And so to Selwyn College, Cambridge in October 1956.

"Of Cars, Cambridge and College Chapel"

Life holds many a strange coincidence. Apart from chums in my "house" at Rossall school, my two main compatriots were Gyde Horrocks and Andrew McKay. Our common bond was motorsport and we shared the expense of buying the motoring journals. Once we had reached the exalted rank of school monitors many is the night we wittered away in deep and meaningful discussions, and what we did not know about cars and motorsport was so insignificant that it really didn't matter.

The first time I was ever spun was by Gyde when his father mis-

Gyde Horrocks seen adjusting things on the Healey 100/6 record car with Marcus Chambers by the front left hand wing.

guidedly allowed him to borrow his Austin 16 one exeat weekend to go for a run. Trying too hard on the Cleveleys to Preston Road he lost it coming out of a long left, and we arrived backwards on the road side grass outside a house which was once the property of George Formby.

These two elected to proceed straight to Cambridge while I went to serve her Majesty. There was no question of Gyde serving as he had been a polio victim a year or two before (causing us all to be at home for the Coronation as school had to be closed) and I do not remember whether Andrew was ever called to the colours or not. He had, however, taken the precaution of creating his own religion which he believed might serve him in good stead. He is the only member of "Jehovah's own seventh day bush veld anabaptists" that I have ever had the privilege to know. The coincidence was that these two were starting their last year when I went up, and both held senior positions in Cambridge University Automobile Club, whose more enthusiastic and thirsty members met with almost alarming regularity in the Bath Hotel, St. Benet's Street. I had paid the odd visit to meetings while soldiering and was quickly co-opted as first year committee member.

I knew no one in the shooting world and as I was and still am rather shy, it was more of an effort to get involved there but my early performances on the range were satisfactory and I soon made good friends. I had kept up my boxing through service life and fought a few times when I first arrived but soon established who would fight my weight for the University and saw little point in being his punch bag, so retired. I hunted once with the Trinity Foot beagles but no one was the slightest bit interested in the two northern packs I had "whipped in" for, or that I had on two occasions actually hunted hounds. What a toffee nosed team of trogs. I sent my beagling gear home and asked mother to prepare it for the Christmas Vac. The ski club was a little similar although some of those could really ski, whereas I had seen little ability displayed on that one day by the hunt officials of the Trinity Foot. Perhaps I was unlucky.

Where to worship is something of a problem to those of that mind in a place like Cambridge which abounds with really live groups of every shade of the Church of England persuasion. However, motorsport and shooting were University based and I felt that I should have some commitment to, and involvement with, my college, Selwyn. This was a relatively new college and a Church foundation, old man Selwyn having been something splendidly episcopal, either at home or overseas. I elected therefore to have at least some involvement in the running and worship of the college chapel, a pleasant place. I little realised what an ace I was dealing myself. I was to read theology and my tutor was a Selwyn man and I would also attend the Principal's church history lectures. It was a "middle of the road'' set up which suited me, no bells and smells, but no ping pong position (minister operating from one end of the altar) or evangelical Hallelujahs. These things I am not necessarily opposed to but do not prefer. For my first year I had digs in college so attendance at daily Morning Prayer and Holy Communion was easy and I joined the short list of servers. Herein lay the ''ace''. Chapel lay on the south side of the quadrangle, the main door within the quad but the body of the building jutting out into the gardens like some sort of brick pensinsula. There was a door from the vestry out into the gardens, for which successive servers had keys. No climbing in after hours for us, just a look of sanctity, solemnity and sobriety as we came out into the quad. It was the look of sobriety which was, on occasion, difficult to achieve. Not that I was late in every night of the week, but because of National Service and continued shooting I was a member of the University Officer Training Corps Mess, which did not seem to be governed by normal licensing laws, and when car club chatter had ended I sometimes wended my way thither for an extra slurp or two, causing re-entry through the vestry to be necessary. As I had elected to ''drop'' boxing I arranged to play some squash and do some running with another theological student, and so the Cambridge scene was set.

I worked hard at the organisational side of the Automobile Club and was soon rewarded with a navigational ride with Gyde Horrocks in his mother's Austin A30. The start was in Derbyshire near Ladybower reservoir at about 5.30 p.m. with a supper stop at Ilkley, then into the Lakes and southern Scotland before finishing at breakfast time and a long run back to Cambridge. We were very slow up hill but Gyde was superb on the descents and we were putting up a very creditable performance.

Somewhere in Scotland on some blasted heath I got out to open a gate and most of the maps blew out. Retrieval was impossible, but next man up was a team mate, Tim Docksey, in a Series E Morris 8. We had to follow him until I was on a map again. A succession of navigational outings followed and as it was always ''plot and bash'' (the route was handed to you on the start line and you worked it out as you went) my early association with ordnance maps was invaluable. I operated in standard eights and tens Austin A35's and A40's and sometimes got a drive. The vehicles were all little more than shopping cars on standard tyres and standard brakelinings. A pencil or two, appropriate one inch ordnance maps, a potty (illuminated map magnifier) and a Blackwell calculator (given two of three, miles, average speed, minutes, the third could be read off) were all the navigational aids one could hope for. A tow rope, spade and pick helve were frequently useful things to have, plus wellies and extra sweaters to cover total submission of motor on some moorland expanse. The pick helve, do I hear you ask? I still carry one, it is the best weapon I know of for lifting a bent wing or wheel arch off a wheel, thereby permitting the aforementioned wheel once more to revolve. A few favourite passes were regularly in use as stages and tie deciders. Hardknott and Wrynose were typical and were simply not "on" either together or separately in an A30 in the dark at 30 mph. However the advent of the Triumph TR2 was to alter all that and organisers, while telling the RAC that the control to start Hardknott was at the phone box and the next one at the bridge on the far side, actually moved the controls further apart to prevent "clean sheets".

Speed and performance, of course, are not everything. I am reminded of two occasions, one an Inter-Varsity Rally. A certain Geoff Breakall, of Loughborough College went tremendously fast in his TR2, but unfortunately his navigator was not quite so fast. Several times we met Geoff going with great enthusiasm in the wrong direction. Our very standard Austin A30 was well above him in the final reckoning. The other time was on some CVAC driving tests held on our favourite dis-used airfield, where much testing took place. It had rained all night and well into the morning, most tests, some of them really rather fast, were drying out. A TR2 was present, it may have been Geoff again, Archie Scott Brown in a very large and lightly modified Mark Two Zodiac and a flotilla of lesser devices. A small Renault was driven by Rod Mansfield, again a school friend of mine, who has risen to be Manager of Special Vehicle Engineering at Fords. The TR2 was driven with gay abandon, the Zodiac with incredible dexterity and precision (Archie had only one complete hand, a stump for the other and two club feet, yet raced in Formula One and Lister Jaguars) and the little Renault chugged round always taking the shortest route between two points. Final result the Zodiac, the Renault and then the TR2.

Witchford airfield, the venue of these tests, and the kindness of friends better heeled than I, allowed me to put to the test all the mental preparation that I had indulged in over the years. I had driven the parental Consul and the Hovis Special but rarely alone. The Consul was preceded by a 1500 cc Singer Sports which was a superb motor with a fly off handbrake. In this I passed my test, and on odd occasions was able to let it loose on my own. But I still had a lot to learn. I had watched and read about people in action in anger and I knew how I would do it when the opportunity arose. The odd rally on which I had driven, I think I took reasonably fast but with respect for the owner of the vehicle who was invariably present. At Witchford there was tremendous undamaging space, little tight sections and vast perimeter track, very fast and in part, out of sight of our "base" area. Here I drove as fast as I wanted to, a Silverstone Healey or XK120, a rather special works D.K.W., a 1500 cc HRG, an MGA Coupe, a Healey 1004, a modified Jaguar 3.4 and

"by a 1500 cc Singer Sports... In this I passed my test". Also my first motor-bike, a 98 cc James max speed 42 mph cruising 38 mph.

a very pleasant Jensen.

I was constantly in trouble at school but only in the lessons I didn't like. It is easier to list the ones I did like in which I was invariably top or second and they were History, English Literature and Divinity. I saw little point in the others. After all, everyone that mattered spoke

English, even my Austrian relatives, I had no intention of becoming a scientist (actually I was barred from Chemistry for causing an unscheduled explosion and from Physics for cooking baked beans on a bunsen burner) and while some basic arithmetic was necessary, to calculate one's horse racing winnings and to convert miles into kilometres, the rest seemed only to be of interest to people who lived in a special sort of cloud cuckoo land. I therefore employed these lessons to mentally prepare myself to drive fast. I studied pictures in the journals of people drifting, sliding, on opposite lock, getting wheel spin off the line, and working out how it all could be caused to happen.

Even at fifteen I understood about weight transfer, whiplash, understeer, oversteer, breakaway point and other relevant theories. The trouble was that this tremendously worthwhile study was frequently interrupted by the high speed arrival of a well aimed board rubber, a clip round the ear or a ridiculous request to decline something or otherwise take some active part in the lesson, which I was invariably unable to do with any show of knowledge or intelligence.

But this private self tuition bore much fruit, for when let loose at Witchford I knew exactly what I had to do and it became embarassing to find that I was frequently faster round the peri track than the owners of the Jensen and the Jaguar in the dry and in the wet (and I put this down to early training on motorcycles). I could take on most comers in most machines. They were heady days, but not everything went right. Our other happy hunting grounds were some gravel pits near Duxford airfield. I had acquired a 500 cc Trials Norton with competition chair and one or two others had trials bikes. After the lunch time pinta we sometimes adjourned to these gravel pits to practice trials riding and scrambling. Everyone got a ride, whether they owned a bike or not and we normally returned full of fresh air, wet, muddy, happy, tired and thirsty. On one damp day I elected to try a very steep little pitch which was normally regarded as solos only. I told my regular passenger, John Aley, to jump clear if I shouted or if he should think we were going to go over backwards, which was the obvious danger. As we neared the top, the front wheel began to rise and John jumped clear when I shouted. I got my boot jammed between bike and chair. The whole outfit rolled over backwards with me on board, taking the weight of everything on my back each time I passed the ground, the motor kept running and petrol dripped from the filler cap onto my chest. After what seemed like hours we arrived at the bottom, on the wheels and facing the hill with the motor still ticking. I looked up at the six or eight horrified faces at the top of the hill, made a snap decision, engaged first and rode to the top and over it, scattering my friends in the process. I stopped, climbed off and collapsed in an undignified heap. I was sore for many days after, and I cannot really imagine why, but I sometimes suffer from back trouble and Sue has to minister to the aches and pains.

During petrol rationing caused by the Suez crisis we ran a trial for push bikes. I organised it and I won it. This bit of totally useless information comes to you free, contained within the price of the book. But it does have relevance. I designed a course to accommodate beef and brawn as well as expertise and the most difficult section, where the most points could be lost, contained a sort of balancing act along a ridge and then a very difficult downhill section. Having organised and ridden in push bike trials in my own village and made my elder sister Su ride through many a water splash, muddy patch and so on, the event was relatively easy for me. But it was the downhill section that allowed me to win. Beef and brawn excelled elsewhere, but expertise, balance and courage down hill won the day. Within a very few years Erik Carlsson was to say to me that he and I were about the two fastest people in Europe, downhill. (I don't think at that time that the rest of the world had been discovered as far as motorsport was concerned. Well, there was the Safari, but really that was it).

From these fairly informal and regular meetings grew some much

"and made my elder sister Su ride through many a water splash".

bigger and more important things. What I have tried to show up till now in this narrative are, I think, the growing pains, pleasures, and pranks of one who dreamed of serious motorsport but perhaps thought that it would always escape him.

I suppose it was inevitable that new ideas should be born, matured, and discussed in the Bath Hotel at luncheon times, and expanded later in the day. It was Gyde Horrocks who was responsible for our first exploit into International Motorsport. We should, he said, break records, long distance records, because all the short ones were held at very high speeds. The International governing body of motorsport has its offices in Paris and there they hold the details of present records in their various classes according to a car's engine size measured in cubic capacity, and also in time and distance. Gyde went to Paris to do some research and came back saying that he thought that class 'G' records for four days and over could be taken on by an Austin A35.

This news was received with the sort of hilarity that it appeared to deserve, however once the dust had settled and the laughter had died down, Gyde produced the details. The records for under four days stood at 86 mph which was not within our reach, but after

"could be taken by an Austin A35". The A35 on the banking at Montlhery.

15

previous page: "Pit signaller" Rupert Jones.

up. At its steepest point a really fit person wearing gym shoes might reach the top in a mad dash. Coming off the banking onto the straight, the road circuit goes off to the right as the second banking begins. As you come off the second banking and stands and pits come into view, the road circuit rejoins from behind one's right ear.

Marcus, plus the BMC mechanics and the superb Abingdon mobile workshop had already arrived, and soon the Le Mans and Loire Valley team docked. It was the 30th June 1957, and the time of the Suez crisis; petrol was rationed and the Alpine Rally had been cancelled. Sufficient petrol for our enterprise had been organised and because there was no Alpine we had stronger Abingdon support than originally envisaged. The mobile workshop was parked adjacent to the service bay and here Douggie Watts, Doug Hamblin (now regrettably deceased) had set up shop and I think never left for the duration. I had never seen the works boys in action before and it was the start of a revelation that was to gradually unfold over the next ten years while my association with Abingdon was maintained.

For speed, clinical efficiency, knowledge, stamina, guts and unending good humour they were a race apart. I have had the

"Gyde... had borne the brunt of the organisation". He takes the A35 away into the night while testing.

privilege of working with all sorts of good teams in school, in church, in the services, in shooting, but none has ever outshone those men.

Surprise, surprise, the weather was so hot that even some of the most hardened members were driven to leave alcohol and take soft drinks. The thermometer was in the 90's all day, every day, and at night never dipped below 80°. One of the favourite thirst quenchers in La Potiniere was the citron pressé, your actual lemon juice squeezed from the lemon into a glass. It makes a quite superb drink under such circumstances and had the added advantage of getting "Madame" into a fearful fluster if one ordered, say a dozen at one time. The track was in regular use by the French motor industry for testing, largely of an endurance nature. Each day the same blue overalled Frenchmen with the same blue berets and the same droopy moustaches came in the same old Citroens (the pre-war type body shell) and hurtled round the track all day at a steady 80 kph or 50 mph. One driver told us that his car had been twice round the clock but of course only in kilometres, and that part of his tests were for bore wear. De temps en temps (well, we are in France now) the relatively new I.D. and D.S. Citroens would appear and proceed at a great pace going high up on the banking, well above our humble A35 and soon were inevitably christened Citroen Pressé.

Circuit tests showed the A35 to be easily capable of sustaining about 80 mph, scrutineering was successfully completed and all was set for blast off on July 1st. I don't think anyone dreamed of a trouble-free run or indeed much in the way of success, least of all it seemed, the drivers of the assorted Citroens and occasional Renault, who, apart from ourselves, were the only sort of "rent a mob" to witness an inauspicious start. Gyde had allocated two of us to each driver as time keeper, pit signaller and additional pit staff. Marcus was nominated reserve driver. The heat continued as the little car left on its first lap of an attempt to do in a week what many regard as a years mileage. We kept our own lap charts for our own interest and just to double check the officials, who always seemed to have us down for a lap or so more than we had recorded.

There were to be two sorts of pit stop, one every three hours to change drivers refuelling and basic checks like oil and water. Flies were a problem and windscreen and lights had to be regularly cleaned, and sometimes the radiator core pressure blown free of frizzled flying flak and flies. This stop we regularly achieved in under one minute. Every twelve hours a longer and more thorough check was carried out. Oil change check on gearbox and back axle, oiling of steering gear and swapping around of tyres, (the off side front took some hammer) were all undertaken in about four minutes. Gyde ordered exercise, we ran round the circuit, some took salt tablets, they were wise. Gyde did not, and also he had borne the brunt of the organisation. On day two he collapsed getting out of the car due to heat and exhaustion. The services of Marcus were called in. The drivers tried to get the best graph for regular lap times over the three hours and therefore required their pit crews to give their previous lap time to the second regularly when they came round. However, the operation soon became pretty boring, so we invented a method of playing noughts and crosses. The signaller made his move on the board and displayed it to the driver. On his next lap he decided on his move and indicated by judicious use of heads, sides and indicators as he passed. The signaller recorded the move and made his own next move before the driver came round again. We also had a blackboard upon which sectionalised messages might be written, some serious, but more often of a humorous nature. "There is a letter for" ..... lap ..... "We have opened it" ..... lap ..... "It is from Gloria" ..... lap ..... "She says" ..... The drivers recourse to redress was a note pad and pencil. The speed was so relatively slow that notes could be written and ejected from the window when passing the signaller.

The windows had normally to be kept shut for aerodynamic reasons, which made the temperature in the car almost unbearable and iced bottles of drink were warm within the half hour. Thermos flasks? No one dreamt of the fiercest longest heatwave for years. We were just not organised for this one. Fire crews working on three hour standby, followed by a three hour shift, allowed eighteen hours off, but sleep and food allowed for, there was not a vast time for recreation. But a swimming pool had to be found and the nearest good one was some half hour away at La Ferté Alais. Thither those not on duty frequently adjourned. Sleep was not easy as the long low wooden hut in the trees was an airless oven of a place. But the pub verandah was the centre, the hub, the nub of social activity and all day and far into the night small groups, expanded at meal times, debated the finer points of motor sport, world affairs and what one should drink with well-hung grouse, oysters or just Lancashire hot-pot.

At the end of day 3 the little motor, including stops had averaged 75.03 mph and it began to dawn on all of us that the first record was only 24 hours away. Controlled tension, excitement and expectation infiltrated the camp and as the hour approached the pool was abandoned and people started nonchalantly to hang around. The fourth day record came our way at 74.9 mph and day five at 74.95, then the 15,000 kilometres at 74.82 and 10,000 miles and six days at 74.79. This showed a rise of some 13% over the previous records. We had one slight setback on day five when a rear spring shackle bolt severed and it took twelve minutes to replace this and proceed. Our last two records were completely new to the record book, the 20,000 kilometre going at 74.89 mph and the seven days at 74.9 mph. The tension and excitement of the early records had gone and the heat had got at everyone, curiously what had sounded something relatively easy physically had turned into torture by heat and boredom.

The last day was enlivened by dramatic rain which flooded the track and caused full throttle to be activated for some six hours, but even this created little enthusiasm and as the final lap was run at 3 pm on July 8th many of the team were away swimming. It was the drivers of the Citroens and Renaults who stopped their tests and cheered and clapped the game little motor home.

Some bonus money was paid by Castrol and Dunlop and in the end none of us lost out financially, and in the autumn a splendid dinner was thrown for us at the Directors' Club. John Thornley, Managing Director of MG, and someone I already knew since my godfather was secretary of the MG Car Club, was present and also that great breaker of records, especially in MG's, Captain George Eyston and of course Marcus was present.

The party was given by Castrol and their competitions manager Jimmy Hill was host. He was looking for a successor and I was able to recommend one of our drivers, Ray Simpson, whose Healey Silverstone I had sometimes driven (surely one of the great post-war sports cars) and similar to the one in which Peter Riley once successfully completed the Liege-Rome, Liege Rally. Ray was making a notably indifferent attempt to graduate sufficiently well in medicine to go onto medical school and follow his father into the family practice. It seemed that Ray might make a much greater success of running Castrol's competitions department. He did get the job in time which explains why in the years that followed, when I made the annual pilgrimage to the Motor Show at Earls Court, I only ever saw the show in the morning after which Ray took me to lunch, rendering much further activity that day fairly null and void. Thank goodness for Turkish baths and or trains to Manchester.

The Castrol dinner was an excellent climax to the attempt. Striking, as it were, while records were hot, Gyde put it to Marcus that Class 'D' 2,000 cc to 3,000 cc records might be taken in an Austin Healey 100 six from 2 to 7 days plus appropriate distances. These were held by Citroen between 86 and 90 mph. One hundred miles an hour for a week became the ultimate goal and this clearly was a much more advanced project than the A35 but it was agreed that the attempt should be made with the proviso that the date be not July but some time when less extremes of heat could be expected. Many of the Austin A35 brigade were still available and we had some excellent new recruits. Since no large finance need be found by us, and as I had by now proved my ability to drive with reasonable competence I was promoted from pit crew to driver. Important people who had slightly pooh-poohed the A35 plan suddenly became almost over-enthusiastic. All sorts of problems had to be sorted, the ideals revs, about 4,000 was not ideal for the motor as vibration might set in. The racing tyres Dunlop wanted us to use at a fairly high pressure would surely wreck suspension and shock absorbers at over the ton on those appallingly bumpy bankings. We were advised not to use overdrive which brought us back to 4,000 rpm. An oil cooler was recommended but apparently one of Marcus' pet hates were external oil pipes, I wasn't sure what these were, but if the alternative was for oil pipes to run through the office I was definitely agin that. We ended up with no oil cooler but running on Castrol R, that delightful smelling oil which will forever for me be associated with Manx Nortons and Vincent Black Lightnings and the like. For drive we ended up using the overdrive and a 3.9 final drive and an engine with two larger than life carburettors, basically the same, I am reliably reminded, as those used for the 1958 Sebring twelve hour race, which no doubt some of you will clearly recall.

The splendid mobile workshop was to attend once again. This had been built originally for the MG racing team in the mid-fifties and provided facilities not only of fettling cars but also for mechanics to cook, eat and sleep and so on. Most of us crossed to France on September 3rd and my journey was considerably more enlivening than that of the previous year in the J.2 van. One of our number, Arthur Taylor, was on his maternal side, one of the Cadbury family, who had some sort of family business based at Bournville. Arthur was quiet, unassuming, very intelligent and large. We were great friends and I had stayed at his family home from time to time. Like myself he was most appreciative of all the good gifts with which God seemed to have surrounded us lucky ones and he and I instituted the Saturday morning "roof top breakfast". Arthur had digs in town some hundred yards or so (the day of the metre, blissfully, had not yet dawned) from our Headquarters, the Bath Hotel. He had a top storey room with access to a flat roof which, in the words of the immortal Gerrard Hoffnung "afforded delightful prospects". The adjacent roof tops, Kings Parade, in parts, Kings College Chapel, the Senate House, and the front door of the Bath Hotel. Here, he and I and the odd very carefully vetted guest would meet at or about 10 am to enjoy fruit, cold chicken, ham, boiled eggs and other delicacies, washed down with black coffee and then the odd bottle of Chablis or Sancerre. Having attended to these small matters, put the world to rights and organised the rest of the weekend, we normally found that the Bath beckoned.

During the long vacation Arthur's family decreed that in order to be the better prepared to proceed to the awaiting desk at Bournville, he should spend some time in some remote African colony, yes, I think still pink upon the world atlas in those days, and see for himself the growing and harvesting of the raw material which was the basis of the family product. This exercise was to take a good two months and Arthur had arranged for his beautiful 1500 cc HRG to go back to the works when he flew out, for a two week overhaul. As those two weeks came to an end I would be at Bisley, just down the road, would I very much mind collecting the Hurg, running it for the summer and producing it at Paris airport to collect him as he arrived from Africa? Would I mind!!

Transport was becoming a problem, to finance navigational outings and the odd drive, my rather attractive stable of motorcycles was rapidly being reduced and soon I should be back on foot if I was not careful.

The Bisley fortnight was fine weather-wise and the first week was the really critical one for my team, the second week was more for fun, so I rang Hurgs to arrange to collect at about 9 am one morning of that second week. Having carried out the checks and done the paperwork I folded the hood, stowed the side screens, lowered the windscreen, so that just the aero screens remained, and fitted the tonneau cover. I could hardly believe that I had nearly two months of motoring in this superb device. I had a good Bisley, recording some success and taking out one or two pals in the Hurg. My "plus four" shooting togs seemed the ideal gear for driving such a motor, but I was glad when the time came to break camp and head for my parents holiday home at Abersoch on the Lleyn Peninsula. On the way I had promised myself something which for me was a pleasant and delightful interlude, a stimulating and yet settling experience which did me a lot of good but would perhaps not be everyone's

"... the first week was the really critical one... the second week was more for fun". Rupert having fun on the 'Running Deer' range at Bisley.

idea of a good way to spend a few days. I headed the Hurg for Oxford, leaving long before "traffic" set out and was through the "dreaming spires" and into the Cotswolds before finding an Inn that was prepared to produce breakfast, over which I dawdled and read 'The Times'. I walked a little and then crossed into Warwickshire and stopped again to take ale and a cheese sandwich. Then I made for the monastery called Glasshampton, not far from Shipston on Stour where the Franciscan friars of the Anglican persuasion used to train their novices. I was expected and was shown to my cell. I had been before and knew the geography, the guest room where guests might converse, for this was a "silent" house except on special days like Easter, The Library, the Chapel, the Kitchen, the Refectory and the vegetable and flower gardens are so beautifully tended by the friars. The rythm of the ordered days, the offices so superbly said and sung in the chapel, the quiet reading allowed during meals, the times for reading and study or strolling and walking in the gardens and surrounding countryside soon soothed the effects of a hectic University year. After a few days I set out across the border into Wales and let the Hurg really go at well known and loved roads that led me to Lamb Cottage and a fond parental greeting. The Hurg was really for me, most controllable when sideways and enough prod to be great fun, this was living. For a week or three I caught up on theology, walked, swam in the breakers at Port Ceiriod, fished off the rocks or from my father's boat and no doubt, drank a little beer in the 'Sun' at Llanergan or the 'Vaynol' at Abersoch. Then it was time to move.

"I took to her at once"
Rupert tries the Healey.

I was to collect Bill Brookes from somewhere near Nottingham. Bill had kindly let me rally his A35 and later his A40 and his father was doctor to a boys Borstal. This sort of work interested me and I was promised a visit. Then Bill and I headed for Dover where several of the team had arranged to catch the same crossing. One was Bill Allday with his 3 litre Bentley. Of course we didn't arrange to have a race, Allday and I, that sort of behaviour could cause loss of competition licenses, but it just so happened that we cleared customs at the same time. First one stopped for fuel then the other, then we had a plug lead come off and Bill took the lead, Bill punctured but changed the wheel in very good time, but not fast enough to prevent me passing him. At the end of a long straight Bill's Bentley was looming ever larger in my mirror, and so intent on watching was I that it was only at the last minute that I saw that the right hander into the next village was upon us. Full opposite lock and the judicious use of a piece of unoccupied market square and we were in the village, Bill arriving in similar style. I waved him down and we decided that honours be shared. Coincidentally (of course) we had come to rest outside a bar, out of which the local male population poured. The cars really turned them on and we were just not allowed to pay for our drinks. We left a lot later at considerably diminished speed, to continue our journey.

On September 4th we were to practise in both daylight and dark, have some official photos taken and test the Pye two-way radio with which VOK 490 was equipped. Marcus arrived pretty well "hot wheel" from the Liege Rally during day time practise. He had

"this booty was carried to the Grandstand". The Healey passes the empty stand, Gyde Horrocks driving.

changed from the rigours of the wooden hut to a bedroom at the Deux Lions de Bel Air, just down the main road. He had to withstand a few barked comments, like did he consider the air of undergraduates to be so bloody Bel, and that sort of thing, but the Liege for crews and accompanying personnel was a devastating experience, so it made good sense.

I had driven a BN4 in a University sprint, but VOK was something different; I took to her at once. She was left hand drive, which upset some, but didn't bother me at all. I was at home almost within minutes and enjoyed the few laps allowed. Some very dim and not even religious red lamps were supposed to indicate the inside edge of the track, but they were virtually invisible, and the headlamps were all wrong. I suppose Marine training had trained me to manage most things in the dark (let your imagination run away with you) and I was the only one not to complain. Headlamps were adjusted which improved the job, but after a few hours of lapping at night I think we could all have managed without any lights at all.

"Headlamps were adjusted". Rupert goes out of the garage into the night.

The Abingdon team comprised of Douggie Watts, Douggie

Hamblin, Gerald Wiffin and Derek Lowe and they, as last years team, never left the track. There seemed to come from the mobile workshop an endless supply of tea, bacon and eggs, all specially imported from England.

The attempt started on time but by evening thunder was rumbling away. However, Marcus left Gyde in charge and retired to his pit with his two sweet smelling Lions. We were lapping at about 110 mph and when real thunder rain set in Bill Summers was driving. Coming off the first banking onto the back straight he must have held her down too low and spun several times, narrowly missing the wall where the road circuit went off. The accident lasted some 400 yards, one of the longest spins in history outside of Bonneville Salt Flats, and Bill came to rest on the grass on the inside. He was shaken but engaged gear and drove to the pits. Two wheels were changed and the attempt continued until clutch slips set in, so we stopped the exercise. It was an error for all it needed was bedding in, but it was changed again and we re-started. We did 30 odd hours and covered 3,000 miles before the rear springs had had it and we

"It was my happy lot to do the last stint". Rupert rather low on the banking.

only had two spares. An old fashioned but excellent idea, provided by Marcus was employed. The springs were well greased, cooking fat being used as we had nothing else and then very firmly bound with whip cord, making the suspension very hard but putting us back in with a chance. Two new springs were flown in, just in time to put one in the car (all spares used during the attempt, apart from plugs and oil filters must be carried on board) before we started again. Time was against us as the circuit was booked for a race meeting the following Sunday. The most we could hope for was about four days. We decided to reduce speed and make sure we took what records we had time for. The two day record came our way at 8 am on September 11th at 98.7 mph to be followed shortly by the 5,000 miles at 98.28 and others followed. It was as well because all we had to show for our efforts until the third attempt was made was a monster party which occurred after the spring failure. We drowned our sorrows at Madame's bar until, quite unreasonably, she decided to shut (it was only about 11 pm) so we pooled all our loose change and exchanged it for red wine and it came to quite a lot. This "booty" we carried to the grandstand along with some food and the odd bottle of duty free which seemed to appear. Between drinks some ran round the circuit and some played cards by the light of the old silvery, which was up and about.

I never did like racing overalls, so when possible, especially for this last stint, wore suit and tie.

Gerry Boxall (now terribly important at Vickers in Leeds causing tanks to be constructed) found himself a bird and was busy on a footbridge. A small posse was gathered together to creep up with all stealth and ruin an otherwise promising enterprise. Shortly before dawn we seemed to have "supped up" and people drifted off to kip.

During Friday night, while Marcus was conducting, a relatively large hole appeared in the second banking which Marcus avoided but hit the concrete that had been dislodged at over 100 mph. He reported in by radio but continued to circulate, so we took transport and went to inspect. Marcus now chose to visit the garage which was bereft of staff (all gazing at a hole in the track) but a French soldier and his girl were much surprised. Unperturbed, Marcus inspected the sump and set out again. Next morning we climbed up under the banking, put an umbrella through the hole and then opened it. Well, it showed where the hole was. The attempt was to end at 2 pm on Saturday and by that time we had added the 3 and 4 day records and 10,000 and 15,000 kilometres and 10,000 miles. It was my happy lot to do the last stint. Quite a few people it seemed would be present when I crossed the line but it was agreed that I should do an extra five laps just to cover any time keeper errors. A goodly little crowd was assembling during the last few laps and as Marcus lowered the flag I launched a toilet roll (cunningly smuggled on board) through the window. In my mirror it was gratifying to see it unroll in quite the approved manner and suitably envelop the assembled company. Some naughty members of the team had also clandestinely suggested that a couple of laps at full bore might be sporting. I managed two laps at just plus of 124 mph before Marcus quite correctly black flagged me. I reduced speed and came in. The Pye radio fell to the floor quite early in proceedings but in spite of the intense vibration continued to work perfectly.

After my quick laps it was discovered that all engine mountings had broken and only really the transmission was keeping the thing in place. After a fairly indifferent start we had still managed seven records and therefore it had been a worthwhile trip.

The car was then successfully raced by Jack Sears and is now the property of Peter Riley who still races her. Another record attempt was to be made the next year, but first to other things.

Cambridge Racing and winter sports

On the Welsh dresser in our living room, along with other pewter pieces, stands an excellent pint tankard with the following inscription:

Rupert Jones
Cambridge Racing 1959
8 Firsts
11 Seconds
5 Thirds

This was presented to me as Chef d'Equipe, or Team Manager, by the drivers at an end of season dinner.

There could have been added to this:- Fifty four starts, fifty two finishes and no mechanical failures. This last being a great tribute to Don Moore of Cambridge, who tuned the engines for Archie Scott Brown's Lister Jaguars, Doc Shepherd's very fast Austin A40 and our three black and shiny Austin A35's. The two non finishes were due to the propensity of one of the drivers to upend his motor. He would enthusiastically dash off on to the grass, yes even at BARC meetings where they had ludicrous rules about not going on the grass (both a childish rule and one ensuring a greater likelihood of accident). Having got nicely off the track and onto the grass, instead of engaging a lower gear and attempting to return to the circuit, he would brake hard while still proceeding sideways. This action is almost sure to invert something like an A35, as clods of earth build up under the wheels so the wheels stop and the body, ever so gently, goes on. Try it sometime.

It was in the Autumn of 1958 that one or two members expressed the desire to go motor racing next summer. Arthur Taylor thought he might campaign in his Hurg, Gerry Boxall would race his sidevalve Morris Minor if he could not raise finds for anything swifter. Brian Whittaker thought his father might come good with some pennies if a sufficient case could be put forward. Although fascinated by the projects there seemed no way I could really join in, for acting as a mechanic is just not in my sphere or realm, although in times past I had stripped and successfully re-built my two stroke motorcycle engines. However after some thought, it seemed to me that if the three were determined to take to the tracks they might benefit by forming a team and deciding on a class to go for and sharing costs. They would need a team manager, to bargain for parts, control preparation, make the entries, get cars to the circuits and through scrutineering and practice, and then sup ale while they dashed about. It took less than several seconds for me to realise that there was really only one person in the club qualified to take up such an important, exacting and influential position. That I had a team to prepare for Bisley and final examinations to take, I felt sure would not really interfere with this exciting and worthwhile project. Later in the day I would call a meeting, I would....... I felt a tap on the shoulder and came back, well perhaps not to earth, but to college chapel. Unnoticed by me Morning Prayer had drawn to a close and I should have proceeded to the altar to assist with the sacrament. With folded hands and bowed head I reverently proceeded to my place in the sanctuary, and one of my lewd friends was unable to restrain a titter of totally irreverant mirth. The wretched fellow is now a Bishop, I am not looking for a job in his diocese. Who wants to live in the South of England anyway?

Later in the day we had our meeting. It took me a while to sketch out my plans and it was agreed that we should all sleep on it, do some sums, talk to parents and/or bank managers and talk again in a few days. In time it was agreed that we should field a team of small saloons in the under 1,000 cc class. The A40 was not yet available although the Cambridge based Doctor Shepherd was

Gerry Boxall in the car equipped with 1.1/2 inch S.U. carburettors, seen here at Silverstone.

promised one for the season, we could not afford either the time or the money to wait. The alternative was the well known Austin A35, for which Don Moore had already given me some prices for preparation, he having prepared last season's class winning car for the good Doctor.

The three owner drivers to be, liked the idea but wanted to talk to Don and also for me to get some prices for new cars and also for parts which we would need. With a good word from Marcus and an understanding dealer we were able to get a fair discount on three new black A35's and arranged to collect them from the factory ourselves. Don had suggested that we try three different sizes of twin SU carburettors. With most other contenders in the class inch and a quarter was the accepted size, but Don felt that while this made for the best all round performance they left something to be desired in terms of terminal velocity. It was agreed that Gerry was likely to be the fastest driver, he had flown high speed jet aircraft for the Fleet Air Arm during National Service, and showed great promise in his side valve Morris Minor, so he won the inch and a half carbs to give him high speed at the top end. Brian wanted the inch and a quarter, and Arthur, gentleman as always, was quite happy to take the remaining inch and an eighth carbs.

However I am rushing ahead. The date for picking up the cars was put off and put off, black was not scheduled to be used just yet, and the date of our first race, inevitably got closer and closer. Then Don chucked the final spanner in the works, he quite rightly said that he would not touch any engine that had not done 5,000 miles. When the cars finally came available they were taken to Witchford to circulate indefinitely around the peri track. Don relented and said, scratching his backside and puffing at one of the small cigars he loved so well, while standing in front of the stove in his workshop, that perhaps 3,000 miles would do. Even so, that was 9,000 miles in total and a great deal of time and petrol money. Each driver chose at least one "mate" and as someone completed a stint he drove back to Cambridge to hand over, and so the process went on. I worked in with Arthur and we chose to do longish stints and then have a reasonable rest period. What work we normally did was temporarily abandoned. Within three nights and two days all three cars were with Don and the appropriate mileage was registered.

I think my real job then began. Don, as all real engine tuners, especially in the days before rolling roads and other fancy gadgets, was an absolute artist. But as with most great artists there is a degree of temperament and being in the right mood for the job. As our cars landed, Archie's Lister was being prepared for testing to be followed by the first race of the season. The A35's stood lonely and unattended as time went by. As two of the drivers, and one in particular, thought they understood about tuning and race preparation, and knowing how Don would react to unsolicited advice, I had made them agree not to go down to Don's. But as the days went by I was having a job to restrain them. The Lister left the shop and was successfully tested. On Monday morning I went down to the shop and Don was standing in front of the stove smoking...... and sometimes scratching. We talked a little, then we stood in silence, then we talked some more, then silence. Then we made a brew and talked some more. Then, quite suddenly he outlined the complete plan for engine preparation, remarked that it was dinner time and said he would start as soon as he got back. He did, and worked until one am next morning. Parts were polished and perfectly matched, valve gear laboriously lightened, individual exhaust manifolds for each carb set up, beautifully and carefully constructed, crankshafts sent to be balanced, these operations filled the next few days. The owner drivers were allowed down once, under escort and at Don's invitation. They said little, but I could tell they were really pleased at last.

I needed one more trip to Abingdon. On my first trip Marcus had instructed Douggie Watts to provide as much as possible for as little as possible. I had on that trip collected largely engine parts. Now I needed springs, differentials, instruments and anything else which might come in handy. When I arrived, in some borrowed transport, a motorcycle and sidecar, seeming not to be quite the right sort of thing on which to arrive at "Comp Shop", I had to play the waiting game, at which through life I have got no better, although I seemed to have some advantage over some people I can think of. When Marcus finally disposed of the impediment he greeted me enthusiastically and apologised for the delay. In fact I had had an interesting and useful walk round and a talk to some of the lads I already knew.

Doc Shepherd had had "springs coil front suspension" specially made up to a particular "spring rate" for his A35 and now for his A40. These were monstrously expensive, but our engineering boys worked out that they were within an ace of the spring rate of those fitted to Sprites and Midgets which came in at two pounds ten shillings each less discount. Marcus was one of those who believed instruments were important, as indeed I do and we agreed on rev counter, water and oil temperature, oil pressure and an ammeter. We were later to have enormous fun mounting these as Ferrari. This I suppose is now common practice for many, but just in case there are those who don't know, when all is well and you are going full bore all needles should be at twelve o'clock. I am just wondering whether I have to work that one out for you or perhaps you can do it for yourselves. I will give you one clue. The "Red" on the rev counter started at twelve o'clock, if your needle got to one o'clock you were well into the red. We drew the line at a "tell tale", that is an extra needle on that instrument which stayed at the highest revs used, for team manager and mechanics to see. Differentials were the other essential. We had learned from the A35 record attempts what diffs were available, and changing diffs is cheaper than changing gear ratios. We needed a really low one for tight circuits, an in between one perhaps for road use and circuits which were both fast and slow, and a long legged one for Snetterton and Silverstone and places where terminal velocity were important. Douggie Watts provided nine diffs, three to suit each requirement, and if memory serves correctly they were four point five to one, four point one to one and three point nine to one. But Douggie was left to sort out the detail.

Proof that I was now "part of the show" and accepted, was about to be amply demonstrated. Marcus took me to lunch at the Dog House at Frilford Heath. This was, and I believe still is, a really delightful hostelry, used regularly in those days by Marcus for entertaining. Occasionally, at special times, we used the Lamb and Flag at Kingston Bagpuize, which was further away, flag-floored and produced excellent food, ale and wine. The Dog House, much nearer to Comp Shop, but with two or three sporting bends and some nice straights, en route, was somewhat more sophisticated. Pints served in pewter pots, carpet covering the floor, a very adequate menu and interesting wine list. Although I was not to discover this on day one, they also always carried a decent decanted vintage port and a splendid Stilton. On this, my introduction to 'The Dog House' Marcus told me many things, about himself and his life, especially times involved in motor sport. He took a keen interest in my plans to be ordained and also my interest in shooting. It was a very worthwhile meeting and when we returned to Abingdon I found my vehicle loaded with the necessary parts plus some unordered ones, which included Riley 1.5 brake drums providing more stopping power. The booty was so good that I allowed the team and Don to get together and unpack our spoils. They were well pleased and when they discovered that our budget would be very little affected their joy was complete. Don stubbed out a practically unsmoked cigar, had a wash and we all went for a drink. Our first meeting was not far off, but now it looked as if we would come under starters orders.

I think our strategy of running three almost identical cars (radiator grills were painted different colours) paid off with race organisers. They seemed glad, when I went up to London with our entries, to receive them, and although I only once extracted starting money I think we were never refused an entry. We were keen to be professional but not pushy or superior, which reminds me of a tale of about these times, showing that this policy can pay. Some four or five of us, led by Tom Threlfall and in his VW van set out during the Christmas vacation for a skiing holiday in Austria. We were to call at the town of Bludenz in the Vorarlberg and look at the cotton mill and brewery which belong to my Austrian relatives and then proceed to a high, and in those days little known resort, Zürs, on the Flexen Pass. On the night boat from Dover were four rather "far back" young men talking rather loudly and drinking scotch or brandy. We took our pints to a far corner. When we came to unload we discovered that they were from the "other place", were potential ski team members (no one had told us that both University teams would be at Zürs) had a new VW car (Porsche engine hinted at) with the latest metal skis on the roof rack. They left Customs before us in a cloud of dust with cries of "See you in Zürs in a few days old boy". We, of course were not potential ski team members, going perhaps more for the gluwein, glokenspiel and good time. Tom drove and I navigated us out of Calais en route for Reims. After a few kilometres the Oxford VW came by at high speed with a flashing of lights and much waving. They had "wrong slotted" (rally language for a navigational error, incorrect turning at a junction, failure to cope with a map and so on) in the back streets of Calais. Our van trundled happily along at about 65 or 70 mph (indicated) which was quite adequate for the headlights which suddenly picked out a rather posh ski stick. We stopped and collected, went a little further to discover a ski and then another and then the Oxford VW having its roof rack re-packed and with a view to retracing steps, or wheel tracks. We were able to save them that bother and they were graciously grateful. We left them re-packing and securing and contrived to trundle, some of our number sleeping soundly in the stern, blissfully unaware of the little drama unfolding in foreign parts. You will have guessed the next bit, yes, Oxford took Cambridge again with friendly waves. Some kilometres were consumed and we had almost forgotten Oxford; daylight should not be too long away and breakfast was rapidly becoming something of a necessity. Then we observed ahead of us, perhaps in the cold early light of dawn, definite indications of an occurrence. A multi lighted camion was parked on the road side and behind it the Oxford VW. The passenger door, creased and crumpled lay in the road between the two vehicles. Oxford had wished to wee, stopped, opened the door without looking and, lo and behold, the camion buffed it. No one was hurt, the camion driver could not be blamed and he left the scene, there being no visible damage to his machine. We were able to supply them with names and addresses of close VW agents from our list, of which they had not thought to bring a copy, and left them to it. We made Bludenz that night, took in the mill and the brewery next morning and were booked into our hotel and out on the slopes for an hour or so before drinkies time. Two days later Oxford appeared with a door that didn't match the rest of the motor. After that they behaved towards us with due decorum.

I had another skiing excursion with Tom with far less amusing results. The Suez crisis was still making fuel difficult but the VW van ran quite well on a mixture of diesel and petrol, so Tom and I thought skiing in Glencoe would be a good idea. No fancy lifts in those days, climb, carrying skis and fit skis when the snow level was reached. We allowed ourselves one "luxury", we stayed at 'The Kings House Hotel' at the top end of the glen. Scottish hotels in those days were "different". I do like toast, made with brown bread if possible, oaten cakes and wheaten biscuits are somehow not the same thing. Porridge in a Scottish country house or castle, followed by the full treatment, Loch Fynne kippers (I really prefer Manx), kidney, chop, bacon, egg, mushroom, fried potato and other goodies, is something up with which one will put, while the piper on the lawn outside makes sure everyone is awake. But porridge followed by the aforementioned cakes or biscuits with some indifferent preserve (no sign of the Coopers Oxford, one good thing to come out of the other place) is really insufficient bodily nourishment for a day attempting to ski on bare heather and laying solid sandwiches (packed lunch made up at the pub) as ptarmigan traps. After day one Tom and I came down to dinner to find a young couple from our University staying for their honeymoon and intending to do some snow climbing. We did not know them but exchanged pleasantries and retired. Returning next day, we noted that the couple did not turn in for dinner. Tom and I were at "coffee in the lounge" stakes when Martin dragged himself through the door. They had fallen badly and his wife of only a few hours was badly injured, high up and attached to an ice axe. Martin was injured but was not for giving up. We made him take some soup, then went down the glen in bad conditions to a bothey where Oxford University Climbing Club were staying. Martin told his tale and they agreed to turn out. Martin insisted on going with them. Tom and I would go on down to the police station and raise the alarm. I now have to show my youthful criticism of those days levelled at people who in fact do a wonderful job. But at this time an unwanted problem had landed in my lap and I needed help and co-operation not indifference and red tape. I wanted the same "get up and go" that I hoped that Tom and I were displaying. The policeman said he could do nothing till I had a body, but I could ring RAF Rescue on his telephone. I know now as a police chaplain that there are certain problems that they cannot take on. However, I was just out of National Service and still doing part-time in the Marines, so I put some faith in a call to the RAF. I spoke to an NCO who was helpful and assured me that they would turn out in the morning. But the problem was now. I asked to speak to his senior officer and eventually got to a Wing Commander. You don't often get the chance as a Second Lieutenant to shout at a Wing Commander but at this point I did. What sort of organisation was he running? Our problem was now, not in the morning, I couldn't believe that any Marine or Army unit worth its salt would wait until tomorrow. He rang off, but in the morning they came and did a great job.

We went back up the glen and started up the mountain, to meet the team coming down. The lass was dead, but her body secured, they could not bring her down that night. We took Martin back to the pub and called a doctor. He was injured but not too badly and the doctor put him out for the night, or what was left of it. In the morning Martin could not move out of bed, would Tom and I contact parents? We went back to the police station and suggested that this was their job. Oh no, but once again I could use his phone. One of the hardest calls I have ever made was to Martin's parents. I suppose the experience has stood me in good stead and both sets of parents were grateful for what we had either done or attempted to do. By now the RAF had retrieved the body, but not without some problems. Tom and I set off south again, older and wiser, I think.

Don was now making good progress with the A35's but Archie's Lister and other customers had to be attended to as well. Between this time and our first meeting was the CUAC sprint at Snetterton. In those days it was traditionally the first speed event of the year. Two years earlier Tom had kindly allowed me to drive his MGA, in which I did not disgrace myself, but somehow the "A" never really suited me. After TD's and TF's the suspension was too soft, and the gear lever too short, so that one could "beat the box". This was corrected in the "B" and was right in the Riley and Wolseley 1.5's which all had a longer gear stick which made for delightful and fast changes.

The following year John Clarke from Bolton kindly let me drive his Austin Healey BN4. John had come "up" to play rugger to college standard, but gradually became more and more involved in the car club. In his first year he had an Aston Martin in which he had a very bad accident and recovery took time. There was an extra embarass-ment as John did not have permission from his college authorities to keep a vehicle at Cambridge, which was necessary in those days. Years before, my father who was at Jesus College, Oxford had applied for permission to keep a motorcycle while "up". I remember seeing the reply on a college crested postcard "Jesus permits one motorcycle".

John did some time without a vehicle and then, when he deem-ed the time to be right, he made application. He had already ob-tained the correctly coloured light blue BN4, and his tutor sent for him. He pointed out the error of John's ways re vehicles in days gone by and then enquired about John's new vehicle. John replied, "Oh just a little blue Austin, Sir." The tutor, delightfully untutored in matters automobile, decided that a little blue Austin sounded safe enough, and allowed the motor.

The course for the sprint at Snetterton still needed to start and finish in the same place as, although we were playing with electronic gear, stop watches were still in use, and a common area for start to finish was convenient. This meant the use of Castrol drums to mark the course and I collected a few, shooting one high into the air and bending the rear wing. I won the class, apologised to John, and was pleasantly surprised when next year he invited me to drive his recently acquired ex works BN6. This time we had electronics, and the start was some distance before the esses, the course went through these bends followed on through Coram to finish before the pits. It was my contention that if the first bend of the esses was taken with due decorum, it was then full throttle to the finish, at least in the dry. As was my custom I walked the course. Practice was run in the wet and timed runs in drying conditions. I really enjoyed the car and felt quite happy with it sideways on plenty of throttle. Two people spectating out in the country were Marcus Chambers and Peter Riley. I later discovered that my drive considerably impressed them.

At the last minute for our first meeting our cars were not complete. Don agreed that help would be appreciated. Gerry and Brian were delighted and were soon up to the elbows in grease. Don said he would finish Arthur's car, so Arthur and I got out of the way. We could not really find anywhere else to go except the 'Bath', to try a beer or two, and much later took beer, cigars and sandwiches down to Don's. By about 1 am we seemed to have cracked it, and we should make our scheduled practice time next morning. Unfortunately I have not kept records but it was a local circuit, either Silverstone or Snetterton, and I think it was Snetterton, which in

"John invited me to drive his recently acquired Healey BN6... Two people spectating out in the country were Marcus Chambers and Peter Riley. I later discovered that my drive considerably impressed them". Through Coram curve at Snetterton in the C.U.A.C. sprint. This drive altered everything.

those days was a super circuit. I drove the "new circuit" in the dark on a Tour of Britain rally in the 70's, oh dear, not the same thing at all. But most changes are for the worse unless one instigates them oneself. The road from Cambridge to Snetterton through Newmarket could be taken very fast indeed at the right time of day, and as practice for saloon cars was nearly always early we usually got a good run, providing it was not delayed by strings of horses in or near Newmarket. After Newmarket there were several long straights and there are some tales told, no doubt both true and apocryphal, of exploits there on. Archie Scott Brown and Peter Riley both towing sports racers on trailers with near identical Ford Zodiacs, were neck and neck at some phenomenal velocity when the appearance of a farm tractor in the distance caused one or other to give way. Certainly one of the three Tommy Sopwith 3.4 Jaguars hit a pheasant on one of these straights which went through the radiator grille and embedded what remained in the radiator. The three black A35s with grilles one red, one blue, one yellow, were much admired and performed satisfactorily. At Snetterton, a fast circuit, we used our "long legged" differentials and it was obvious that Gerry's one and a half inch carburettored car was the faster at the top end of the range. But contrary to expectation Arthurs inch and an eighth aspirated motor consistently out performed Brians inch and a quarter car, and seemed to hold Gerry's car up into the sixties. Using the cars on the road as well as on circuits we soon found it necessary to put a white stripe down the centre of the bonnet to make it easier for oncoming traffic to judge our speed. Few people expected Austin A35's to be cruising in the eighties and the stripes had the desired effect.

We thoroughly enjoyed our motor racing although personally I was always relieved when scrutineering was over. Don was rarely at the same meeting as we were, and it was often my lot to see one or all of our cars through, and my technical knowledge is easily stretched to its maximum. However we rarely had any bother as our cars always complied, and were produced as clean and tidy as prevailing weather permitted. Things fell into a pattern. If Doc Shepherd was present we came second, third and sometimes fourth. If "The Doc" and the Speedwell A35, driven either by John Sprinzel or Graham Hill, our best car would be third. Both these cars could outpower us and the Speedwell car was brilliantly driven, whether it was Graham or John in command. When we came north to Mallory, Oulton or Aintree there was Harry Ratcliffe, with his very fast Morris Minor to contend with, and Harry knew the northern circuits very well. There was great friendliness within the class and amongst all the saloon car drivers. John Sprinzel, Graham Hill and Jack Sears who raced one of the Sopwith Jags, always called at our camp for a friendly chat and a word or so of encouragement. There

"When we came north ... there was Harry Ratcliffe with his very fast Morris Minor to contend with". Later Harry Ratcliffe and I were to be much involved together in motorsport. Harry in action.

were others too, Billy Blydenstein who conducted a Borgward with great ability, was another friendly chum.

Some team members seemed to take their examination preparation more seriously than I, which was to my advantage, as I got the odd drive, which I thoroughly enjoyed and performed reasonably well. At one Snetterton meeting I made a very good start from the front row outside of the grid, and led even the one point five class boys into the first corner, and held the lead into the Norwich straight, when prod took over. I also seemed to take Paddock bend at Brands better than some. Perhaps it was because I was not afraid to use the grass and keep my foot down if I found it necessary to use the aforementioned greenery. There was one glorious race at what was really "our" circuit, Snetterton, when the main contenders where absent and given a clean run we should get first, second and third in class. As usual we were combined with the fifteen hundred cc. cars and were as fast or faster than many of them. The result was that Gerry was up front mixing it with the bigger cars, Arthur not far behind him, and Brian well ahead of the the other thousand cc. cars. I wanted to do a "Neuauer"and bring my cars across the line as a one, two, three in echelon. How to get the message was the question, and only a couple of laps to do it in. We managed some sort of message on the board, and Gerry gave us a naughty signal, something about coming second, Arthur lifted off and began to allow Brian to close. Next time round Gerry got the message "obey orders" and came to heel. They did it beautifully coming out of Coram in line ahead with a good gap behind them, and then formed echelon to cross the line.

"Some team members seemed to take their exams more seriously than I... I got the odd drive". I made a good start from the front row outside position..." Arthur Taylor is also on the front row in TVE 771, the third car behind is Billy Blydenstein's Burgward.

Bisley that year, just following on from finals and a May Ball, was a personal disaster. My coaching ability was not impaired, but I became what is known as "gun shy". All it means in the initial stage is that one involuntarily closes the operative eye when pressing the trigger, and my scores, especially in the prone positioned non-timed shoots, were not impressive. I could still do rapid fire events quite well but I had to drop myself from my own team for some events and concentrate on coaching.

Bisley was followed by Officer Training Corps camp near Thetford for a week. I was due back in Cambridge the night before my results would be announced from the Senate House steps. However, as I was about to leave camp one of the theology dons who was a Captain in the Corps, arrived for week two. As I held his car door open for him he said, "Well Rupert, I can't tell you more, but we have managed to pass all the brethren this year". So at least I had got a degree. In fact I seemed to have done quite well, and shortly the team left Cambridge, all with end of year results, to race at Aintree and then to take a break at my parents bungalow in Abersoch. Only four or five of us were in the first wave at Abersoch as parents were in residence over the weekend. Father, having heard my results, and not having a light blue flag handy, had hoisted a pair of jeans as well as the Union flag, that of St. George and the Welsh dragon.

Parents were only present at weekends and about twelve of the gang came for a few days at different times. At maximum we were seven and I was in charge of cooking. I think that my attempt to cook fourteen pounds of beef was effectively very successful, it was just trying to relieve the oven of the joint, without spilling the fat, after several pints of 'The Sun's' best bitter.

Arthur was there with his Hurg. John Aley, who was not a member of the University, but had helped our team manage the record attempts, and as he gradually gave up his ridiculous aquatic activities joined more and more with us, had come along with his VW. There was a glorious lane down to the golf course, the beach and the mooring where my father's boat was kept. Going back up to the house made a wonderful hill climb and at 1 am surely no one else would be using it? All went well until Aley went off and collected the dustbin of our friendly farmer and ex-wartime Marine, Griff. The noise of the bin rolling down the hill was, well, noisy, and unfortunately Griff was not amused. However he responded well to some scotch, a generous contribution to a new dustbin and the offer of some help with fencing.

John Aley was the "Man from the Pru" during the week and having taken an important part in our record breaking, would take over Cambridge Racing from me when I went down. John, although only a little older than us was largely bald with a charming face which was sort of adaptable. This becomes important later on. But John, because of his motorboating activities thought he knew about sailing. I know that I don't, and during this holiday had taken my father's boat out only on the engine and we had successfully caught mackerel and sea bass. (No, they don't come in barrels). John insisted on a sailing outing. We set out quite successfully, clearing the Life Boat slip, sailing to the west of the sandspit buoy and east of Chapel Island, (better known to some as Puffin's Island, because in Mother's younger days Puffins inhabited it) and out towards the open sea. I said "John, the half tide rocks, which I showed you on the chart, are dead ahead, about a quarter of a mile (not nautical)". It quickly became apparent that John could not change direction and we were making quite good progress. He lost his normal jolly happy smile. We sailed on. I left it fairly late and as it was about half tide, the water was beginning to break over the rocks.

John was now an unpleasant colour. I told him to drop the sails and went below and started the motor and as we "drove" round the rapidly appearing rocks two super sea lions and some seals flopped onto them. We used the motor in future.

I headed north to Abersoch for a while. I was just getting into a gentle but pleasant routine, a round of golf with Mother, a little fishing from Father's boat, swimming and running to keep fit, beer with the locals, beer with Father, beer with various friends of my childhood whose parents had places adjacent, when the phone rang shortly after breakfast, and while Father was issuing the day's orders (It was rather dull for him when Mother and I were the only available soldiers).

It was Peter Riley. Was I free to do the Liege with him in a works Healey in four weeks time? Was I free! If I was not I would be, but why and wherefore and, and..... Peter unravelled the story. He had driven for Fords recently, but Marcus had put it to him that there were not many who either could or would tackle Healeys but Peter might be one, and if a car became available did he want it? Peter had completed the Liege-Rome-Liege in a Silverstone Healey, in the days when the event went to Rome, and he would certainly drive a Healey and particularly in the Liege. Peter had gone to Abingdon along with a motoring journalist, who was to co-drive, to try the car. Peter had a go on the lanes round Abingdon then put the co-driver Richard Bensted-Smith, in the hot seat. Dickie set off in fine style but shortly lost the car. Peter tells the story so delightfully that it is a shame to try to write it down, but it goes something like this:- "I realised that we were going to spin so I got below the scuttle. The front hit one bank then the back the other. I came up for a look and appreciated that the accident was not over, so went below again. Front to the banking, back to the banking again and I knew that the steering was broken, but Dickie was still on the bridge fighting with the useless wheel. The little pirouette was completed for a third time and we came to rest." Dickie decided that Healeys were not for him, made his apologies and left for his journalist's desk. The car could be rebuilt in time for the event, but a co-driver who could cope with Healeys was required, and I had impressed at Snetterton in John Clarke's car and in the record attempt. I would get £50 for turning out and £10 a day expenses, and could I go down to Peter's for a couple of days tomorrow, time was short?

I put the phone down and gazed out across the bay to the yacht club and beyond to Llanbedrog Head and Pwllheli. So dreams could come true. Peter telephoned again, I was to bring my passport and be prepared to go up to London to get a visa from the Yugoslav embassy. I rejoined my parents, and failed to be nonchalant. "I've got a works drive in a Healey on the Liege Rally." Mum said "Oh well done, darling." Dad said "You can't afford to play about with cars, why don't you stick to bikes like I did?" When I told him that it was all expenses paid and there was a fee for going and that bonuses would be paid for success, he was really thrilled and observed that as it was not yet opening time I had better go to the garage for a bottle of champagne which was, with other "keep cool" drinks, stored under a damp spinnaker.

I left early next day to get to Peter's parents' home on the edge of the Cotswolds in time to get some work done before luncheon. Peter had all the maps and the appreciation of the event in all its stages from our team leader, Chief Constable John Gott. John, after a successful time with HRG's and Frazer Nash, inluding winning two Coupes des Alpes, and a long standing friendship with Marcus had joined the Abingdon team in the early days and was team leader for six years. His knowledge of routes and times was considerable and his notes painstaking and thorough. Peter had his own system of a postcard for each section and each section was colour coded, red for very fast, green for fair to fast and blue, should have time in hand. Road numbers, place names, intermediate and cumulative distances were carefully listed below the coding, and the whole lot kept on the dash board in a bulldog clip, so that both crew members could easily read the top one. On a blue section when one could sleep, the other could navigate, calculate times and drive, thereby allowing each to get a little rest. Although the route changed, the pattern for the Liege did not. It was a motor race in the best traditions of the old town to town events, thinly disguised as a rally. It involved some 3,000 miles, 90 odd hours, an overall average of some 45 mph, and run about fifty per cent on unsurfaced roads. There was little or no official rest, the longest and only stop on one event being four hours, and the following year this was reduced to one hour. There was no restriction on modifications or the use of prototype or special cars, scrutineering being delightfully simple, purely to check for safety and ensure that one came back with the same engine block. There was never sufficient time for major rebuilds. I was to attempt this event five times and finish three, and I never remember more than twenty per cent of the entry finishing, therefore finishers awards were much cherished. The event was run by the Royal Motor Union of Liege and all controls are manned by their members. The most excellent Clerk of the Course was Maurice Garot and he was the architect and orchestrator of this remarkable event. Apart from having a stout motor and a stout heart, to have any chance of success one had to understand the mind of the man. The rally called the Liege-Rome-Liege, first of all did not start from Liege, but Spa, home of a wonderful road racing circuit and of some of the finest cooking in the Ardennes, and Cuisine Ardennes (if that is the phrase I want) may well be matched, but to my mind, is unsurpassed by any in Europe. The next little Maurice Garot gimmick was to start cars on the hill in the town centre leading out to Malmedy, three abreast at three minute intervals. There were those who in the spirit of "last to the top of the hill is a sissy" managed to go straight on into a field. The event also bore the title "Le

Marathon de la Route'' and I think this is an apt description. Some years before my time the straight drag to Rome and back had become too easy, and by now Rome was no part of the event which found its ''meat'' in the Dolomites, northern Yugoslavia and the various French Alpes, such as Maritimes, High Provence and just ordinary High Alpes. The quick will readily appreciate that to achieve this mixture the Dolomites must probably be attempted twice. Maurice Garot had to persuade the governments of five countries that it was really a rally that he was running and not a road race. For this he used two devices. He presented to the authorities a list of ''ideal times'' to be aimed at by competitors. These were all realistically slow. To the competitors he issued this list plus a list of opening and closing times of main controls. Thus if you added up you ideal times between Liege and Zagreb, you would find that the control had been closed for two and a half hours, and you were therefore out. The Yugoslav authorities were not worried, so here ideal times were tightened up and some sections were near enough impossible. Only an hours lateness was permitted and time lost was cumulative. In other words if you lost ten minutes on one section, you started the next ten minutes late; sixty minutes came up all too quickly for many, especially if physical fatigue or mechanical malfunction had set in. In France some passes were closed to the public so very fast times were set.

The other ''device'' used only occasionally was the neutralised section. Austria insisted on being ''neutralised'' as they, at that time, did not love motorsport, and this was good as it allowed time for washing, eating, and car fettling and there was no catch. However in Italy some main road sections, busy with holiday traffic, but for us connecting two vicious passes, were also ''neutralised'', thus making the passes into timid climbs without it showing up in the regulations. It was thus essential to make the best possible time at all times, not to catch up on eating or maintenance, but to stay in the rally, never mind do well.

So this was the recipe as Peter spelt it out to me. The Healeys had the new 3,000 engines in them, it was Pete's first drive for the team, my first international, we just spent the next few hours and days absorbing maps and making our own route plan. We went to Abingdon for me to take our recently re-built motor out, which I did with great reverence and care, remembering Dickie's demise. They were not a beginner's car, the straight cut gears requiring double de clutch and the use of neutral both up and down the box, but the overdrive on second, third and fourth was a great delight, although some felt that this should not be overworked.

I went to London to sort out my visa and meet a few pals, and while there discovered that I should have been attending a ''long vac'' or summer term at my theological college, Wells in Somerset.

I had just assumed that one turned up at the start of the academic year, late September or even better early October after a little stag bothering in Scotland. I telephoned the Principal to acknowledge my transgression, and he said that as I had a degree in theology, it really didn't matter. My acceptance to that lovely college was, I suppose, fairly typical of the workings of the Church of England. After mid-morning service one Sunday at Selwyn when the Principal of Wells had preached a superb sermon, the Master of Selwyn waylaid me and said had I considered a theological college at which to prepare for my ministry. I had not. He pointed out that Wells catered particularly for older men and graduates, especially those from Oxbridge, and suggested that I call at his Lodge for sherry and speak with the Principal. We talked about this and that and he ended by saying that he would be delighted to have me at Wells in 1959, and perhaps I would confirm in writing to his secretary that I intended to enrol.

From London I went to Cambridge as the A35's still had a meeting or two to attend, and I also needed a few things for the forthcoming international. Archie Scott Brown's mother, Jay, was helpful to Archie's friends and had a spare room which was offered to a chosen few, and I had been invited. She wanted to know what everyone was doing and all my news. The next day I displayed with quite incredible dexterity my total misunderstanding of things mathematical. I have previously described the function of the Blackwell calculator. I rushed into the appropriate shop to see our friendly men who supplied such things, and brandishing my Blackwell, said that as I was going rallying abroad I now needed one in kilometres instead of miles. The kindly soul did his best to explain that my existing one would do, but he failed. Eventually the patient fellow took mine to the back, put some white tape over "miles" and wrote on it "kilometres" and returned it to me. A great light dawned, and thanking him I retired to find a dark corner in the Bath. The days went by quickly and after another visit to Abersoch I went to meet Peter at Abingdon and set out for the Southend to Ostend air ferry.

My First Liege

The Headquarters of the Royal Motor Union of Liege was situated in a beautiful building which was part of a crescent, pretty much in the centre of Liege and we parked the Healey nearby in the street with many other entered cars. We went in to the impressive building to collect any latest information or messages, had a quick drink with people Peter knew and made the short walk to our hotel, the "Moderne", and found our room. We soon met up with Marcus and the rest of the team and crossed the road to a delightful little restaurant to sample mussels, followed by steak and then some quite astounding pudding (sorry, sweet), cheese, then brandy and cigars seemed to follow, and I was making several new friends very fast. The team was made up of John Gott, with Ken James from Liverpool (I had met him before) Jack Sears with 'Autocars' sports editor Peter Garnier, Gerry Burgess with Sam Croft Pearson and with Peter and I, all in Healeys, and Pat Moss and Ann Wisdom in a very special Austin A40. Most of these attended that dinner and I was quickly made to feel very much at home and part of the team.

Tuesday was spent in final car preparation, getting last minute route changes, comparing notes with other team members, looking at Liege, other competitors and their cars, drinking a little and eating quite a lot. There would be a scarcity of time for food once the event started.

On Wednesday morning scrutineering took place in a very friendly and informal atmosphere. Most crews had already completed documentation, (showing competitition licences and insurance certificates) and so it was purely noting of chassis and engine numbers by the authorities. In most years this took place in the superb courtyard of a city centre palace, but on this occasion a park by the river was selected. Many of the big names in rallying were there but also some Liege specialists, people for whom this was their one outing of the year, some of them husband and wife crews, and these specialists were not to be underrated. Also present were many of those who ran the controls and took the same controls each year, several people doing more than one control and doing their own bit of private rallying to get from one to the next. For everyone, marshalls, competitors and service crews the next few days were

The Bear and the Bishop, thoroughly scrutineered are ready for battle.

going to be a real challenge, a great adventure and very hard work and it would be some weary folk who made it back to Liege on Sunday.

At 6 pm on Wednesday evening, all competitors having been formed up in running order outside the Motor Union building in Liege, a high speed convoy, led, flanked, and followed by police on Harley Davidsons with flashing lights and sirens wailing, left Liege and proceeded the thirty five kilometres to the centre of Spa, where cars were placed in Parc Fermee. Crews went to eat and consume soft drinks, but butterfly tummies left many a meal unfinished. The tension built up, music from loudspeakers drowned conversation and floodlights came on. There were plenty of spectators, gazing at the rally cars, supporting the bars and just making merry. Ten o'clock drew nearer and the early numbers were allowed to their cars. The first three cars came to the line, the music faded and the commentator took over with a brief history of each driver and co-driver. The crowds round the start line and up the road, to me, the new boy, seemed huge; years later I was to see far larger crowds, in Bucharest, in India and other places. The countdown for the first three, the roar of exhausts and a squeal of tyres and the 1959 Liege

was underway. The tail lights vanished at the left hander at the top of the hill and the sound died away, but already the next three came forward and the commentator was in business again. I had met autograph hunters before, but very few, now they were legion. Apart from Jack and Peter, our team mates would all be away before us. Pat made a fabulous start with the A40 beating a Porsche and gull winged Merc. to the top of the hill. Suddenly having seen this display, I was ready to go. Both Pat and Ann had been very kind and helpful in assisting "The Bishop" as they already called me, to join the team. I was determined not to let anyone down. But I was new to the top end of the game and I would need, and indeed got, an enormous amount of help from Peter, already christened "Bear". It was time for "Bear" and "Bishop" to join their Healey and set out.

"It was time for the "Bear" and the "Bishop" to join their Healey and set out". The 'three abreast' start was a 'crowd draw'. At this stage there was no hurry, but most competitors gave value for money and squirted their motors away in fine style".

There was a Japanese team. It must have been one of the first in rallying and I do not remember which company they came from, but they, crew and car, were meticulously turned out, almost too beautiful. The cars were very upright and perhaps not really rallyworthy. After the first few kilometres there was a timed five kilometres test, a tie decider. Here one of the Japs rolled. Peter and I avoided them and wondered whether hari kari was about to occur.

Now a longish navigational might set in, on Michelin maps, to which I was not really accustomed, with Peter's help I managed. Before dawn we were at Karlsruhe and joining the autobahn to head for Austria. Some quite experienced crews got this wrong and headed north, wasting valuable time. Dawn broke by the time we came off at Neu-Ulm and Peter and I found a cafe, just off route, for a wash, shave and some food. Others, less fortunate slept or dozed in their cars until it was time to book out.

A pleasant run through southern Germany, Austria's Vorarlberg and part of the Tyrol followed, normal traffic being the only hazard. We were to enter Italy via the Reschen or Resia pass, depending on whether you prefer German or Italian. Peter and I took a short break at Bludenz in Vorarlberg to speak to my uncle Rupert, who ran part of the family cotton mill and years ago had spent some time in the Rochdale area to learn "cotton". He produced some excellent unsweetened bilberry juice which was a welcome change from Lucozade which curiously was already beginning to pall. We were early before the Reschen control and made a pretence at bathing in a mountain stream, an activity highly commended by Chief Constable, Gauleitter, John Gott, our ruse worked because we were complimented when we met him at the control.

Now it was to be all systems go, but not quite so "go" as it might

"In Bormio a left turn headed us for the Gavia, surely a real drivers' pass". The "Bear" and the "Bishop" in action.

have been as we got a directive that the Croce Domine pass, the last of the "famous four" was out. Peter said that this could be good, as it was very rough indeed, and it was too soon to start hitting the car hard. Soon we were storming the forty nine lyeets of the Stelvio, Peter working hard, using mostly first, second and second overdrive with odd bursts in third. The weather was brilliant but still some snow decorated the off course scenery near the summit. We set out fast down the gentler side approaching a set of tunnels. Peter was telling me how even in high summer there could be ice in these tunnels, and that a year or so ago Willie Mairesse had spun his Merc, and so we nearly followed Willie's example. In Bormio a left turn headed us for the Gavia, surely a real drivers pass. No tarmac as on the Stelvio, good smooth dirt, some very fast corners and big drops with only a hint of of a retaining wall, it needed ability and confidence to power a twitchy great beastie over this in good time. A right turn at Ponte di Legno on main road (neutralised of course) towards Edalo and left towards the Vivione, loose steep and tighter turns than the Gavia, with very high drops near the top. Tommy Wisdom and Rauno Haltonen have both had "oops nasties" up there in those heights.

After those splendid passes we started on a high speed dash across northern Italy, mostly on side roads to reach Trieste during the night, and cross over into Yugoslavia. Crossing into a Communist country always gave me the creeps, a feeling of utter helplessness in the face of armed authority. On this occasion there was no problem but on another event my Bible and Prayer book bound as one book came under very close scrutiny. In those days Bible smuggling was an important part of Christian mission to help our now recently liberated brothers and sisters in those countries.

We looped into the Pula pensinsula and on to Rijeka and then down the coast. At Serj we turned left into the mountains and tarmac was gone for many miles. High up in the mountains, with no inhabited buildings in sight, we came across two gypsies with a bear on a chain. We might have been in another century. Peter said, "Think of something you know well, your bedroom at home or something like that, does it seem like another life?". Yes, it did, like a dream, and we had not been going forty eight hours yet. After a long, hard and dusty section we came to run up a valley and the general view was that this section should not be too hard. Peter seemed a bit tired and we were not seeing many other competitors, which is sometimes dispiriting. We did however know, being in the eighties out of ninety seven starters, that many people were either out or impossibly late. Peter asked me to drive and made me promise to wake him if I was not happy. He said he definitely wanted to be woken at such and such a point. We were working inland and gradually north again. Peter got his head down and I felt my way fairly gently to start with, then when I had my eye in and was sure that "Bear" was asleep I checked watches and distances and warmed up the pace. The shale rattled against the wheel arches, and the gears, which I had now really tamed, came easily as required. Peter told me later, that at some point he had wakened, realised that I was motoring on, looked at me through half closed eyes and seeing that I was happy and relaxed, decided to continue resting. I thought he was still asleep so went on beyond the suggested point, until we were quite close to the next long and very tight section. I found somewhere to stop and put Pete in and we made our meeting with the service lads near Ogulin, I think. We had some ten minutes in hand, took petrol on board and let the boys do a thorough check over while we swigged Lucozade and ate some cold chicken and cold soup. They told us that Gerry and Sam had gone out quite early on after a minor shunt, that John and Ken and the Girls had gone through going well. Jack and Peter were behind us. Fewer than forty cars had gone through.

The next session was unadulterated graft and dust in both departments. The road surfaces (if road is the right word) were appalling, dust got in everywhere and speech became almost impossible, I gave directions with hand signals, and we were getting very bruised from the constant battering by bits of car. Overtaking (not often, thank goodness) was a nightmare. The only thing to do, it seemed to us, was to force your way through the dust right onto the tail of the car in front. Here there was a clear dust-free "V" and the road ahead could be briefly seen. When a straight occurred, lights on and air horns trumpeting (the number two had a foot operated switch for these latter) one pulled out into the dust and blasted through, hoping there was no unforeseen rock outcrop. The torture stopped somewhere near Lubljana and we booked in knowing that at least another dozen cars had all too literally bitten the dust on that last section. Peter maintained that most of those who got out of Yugo would have a good chance of finishing. There was a main road run to Kranjska Gora (main road is a relative term) and then the passes Moistrocca and Predel back into Italy. We had hoped to do these in daylight but as we left the line it was headlamps on and shortly it was dark. Peter made a good climb and started down well. With four corners to go before joining the fairly easy Predel, we overcooked on braking for a hairpin and collected the retaining wall. The steering was bent and a wheel needed changing. Peter was convinced that we were out, but I persuaded him to drive to somewhere where we could change the wheel and then try to make Tarvisio where we knew we had service. It seemed to take ages but Jack and Peter came through and promised to have the lads lined up to receive us. They did a good job in record time and while Pete thought the steering not perfect at least it was safe and we were in the race again.

There followed a "number two to drive" section, with only two turnings that must not be missed. We said we would lead Jack and Peter Garnier while both drivers got their heads down. We made the first turning but unbeknown to us Gotty and Ken had missed it. Gotty woke to find his car with Ken going well a good twenty minutes off route and they had already lost some time. Although their situation was hopeless John drove magnificently to try and retrieve the sitation. They went past us at phenomenal speed, which was the first clue we had of their problems. I did a quick sum and knew that they were out at the next control, so that left Jack and Peter, ourselves and the Girls still in play. I got very sleepy in spite of taking dexodrin and drynomil tablets. We came to a section where I knew there were two level crossings. I stopped for one and it vanished. I pinched myself and set out again. Peter Garnier flashed his lights and I indicated all well. The same thing occurred just down the road, so I determined to drive straight through the next one, but when I got there Rene Trautmann's Citroen was waiting, so I stopped again. There was then no crossing and no Citroen. Hallucinations, I had heard about them. Peter woke, and Garnier dashed forward. We changed places in both cars, number ones having had some sleep. It was Dolomite country again and then through day three we trekked towards the French border and the last night. We gathered that there were only about twenty crews still running and that some of those were groggy themselves or had groggy machinery. It really was survival of the fittest and life consisted purely of the noise, the long red bonnet, the road ahead and endless times and turnings. We had lost interest in food but Lucozade went down really well, also glucose tablets and in my case Allen and Hunberries blackcurrant thingies which became known as the Bishops Vice. I wish that was my only vice today. We crossed into France by the Col de Larche and there was still some daylight to play with. The evenings entertainment began with the Col d'Alles, known by some crews as the bloody Alles. I believe it is some sort of beauty spot for those with time on their hands, but for rally crews it was perhaps one of the hardest which to put in a really good time, and the last night schedule was very tight. The Col de Huitel and the other minor ones followed. Navigation and driving were at a premium, eyelids were like sandpaper and throats dry. Jack and Peter made a navigational error somewhere in this area and were out, and the Girls although going splendidly were losing time. The Liege was just not a small car event. The final section to count was something called the St. Jean circuit near Grenoble to be transversed twice. It was tarmac in parts and deep loose shale others, steep and wooded and navigationally difficult as some forest roads seemed not to be on the map. An Alfa went off and caught fire and Pete and I were afraid it was the Girls, what we did not know was that their race was run. The gallant little A40 had thrown a con rod. When we reached the control David Hiam, Dunlop's rally chief met us to say that we were the only BMC car still running. The race was over, but there was still the long haul back to Liege and we were both dead beat. David, with whom I became very friendly, promised to convoy with us at least until daylight had properly set in.

Just while we got over the incredible tiredness that came with knowing that the pressure was off we drove twenty minute stints, stopping at one point to walk barefoot in a dewy field to try to waken us up. After a while we were back in business and we let David go on ahead as we kept strictly to the schedule. We had no idea that no one else bothered. As we got to the Ardennes we discussed stopping for a meal, trout were advertised everywhere and the idea of trout and white wine appealed. We stopped, put in some petrol and had the car cleaned, then cruised gently on without a care in the world, oblivious that our world waited for us wondering why we were being so long.

The Spa circuit was joined at the Stavelot corner and going the wrong way towards the start and finish, up the hill through the

"There was a big crowd waiting, huge bunches of flowers ... The last car home but tenth overall out of fourteen finishers" and first in class. Peter, Rupert and SMO 744 tired but triumphant.

woods and onto that down hill, up which we had roared some ninety hours before. There was a big crowd waiting, huge bunches of flowers were presented to us by Maurice Garot's daughter and Maurice himself greeted us, the last car home but tenth overall out of fourteen finishers, and winners of the class for three litre Grand Touring cars. Marcus was very pleased with us, and David Hiam produced a large cigar for me, and lit it, but there was no time to talk as, apart from us, the other finishers were all lined up ready for a smaller but equally high speed well policed Harley Davidson type convoy back to Liege (hit at evening rush hour) to park up again outside the Royal Motor Union. Drinks all round were the order of the day, but soon we went back to the Moderne to bathe and change. Peter, Marcus and I with one or two others crossed the road for a meal, I remember enjoying the mussels and coping with some veal, but tiredness and a few drinks were soon taking over. I slept for ten hours and others for a bit longer. I went to the Club just to see the results in print and found that we could collect our car. By the time I got back others had surfaced and we had breakfast. The prize giving and dinner were that night at a country club type place outside Liege. It was a great evening and a wonderful end to my first international and before Peter and I left Marcus was making noises about the "Bear" and the "Bishop" doing the Monte.

The use of drugs, to stay awake, and in some cases also to go to sleep was quite common at this time. I believe most people were properly advised by a doctor, and certainly, in my case, after I had done two internationals I carried out quite extensive well supervised medical tests on various available "wakeys". There were those who would have nothing to do with them, and John Gott was one of those. My next Liege was to be with John and in deferrence to him I didn't take my wakeys with me. Something happened which I will recount later which helps to make some comparison of the advantages and disadvantages of these things.

I think most drivers of those days could tell the odd story of mild hallucinations. I know my godfather who did the Monte in a Ford V.8. Pilot circa 1949 suffered from them. One three up crew in that year were all convinced that there was a man sitting on the bonnet, but when they stopped he had vanished. Peter Riley on the Routes Nationales in France was regularly plagued by A.A. men who came out from behind the poplars and then ran down the headlamp beams till they vanished into the night, only to hide and re-appear again. On one RAC in Scotland all the post boxes for me looked like policemen and very dour and fierce are Scots policemen, so I kept slowing down until they were established as post boxes. It is amazing what a tired mind and tired eyes came up with.

Every rally has its special appeal and after every Liege one heard people, and particularly Pat Moss, say, "Right, that's my last, I'll never do another Liege''. The following year they were all there again. Of course it couldn't be run again, there is more traffic, rally cars have progressed tremendously and so there are too many differences, but the Liege will always have a very special place in my memories, but perhaps that was partly because it was my first international. I was with a truly great team under a superb team manager and no one could wish for a better tutor, coach and friend than ''Bear''.

The First Monte Minis

I came back from the Liege with some money, or at least some money was due in terms of bonuses for our class win, and I pointed out to Daddy that I was the only member of a works team who was car-less. With the sale of the last motorbike, some of the bonus money and a parental contribution a rather second hand Thames van was acquired and still some pennies remained in the kitty. Another change, although of less importance, took place at about this time. My target rifle, a twenty first present from my parents, was exchanged (with their consent) for a stalking rifle. I still have it, although second hand when I got it, it is still a superb weapon. It is a .275 Mauser, light to carry, accurate to 200 yards and hard hitting. I had already done quite a lot of stalking, roe deer and red deer in Scotland and roe and chamois in Austria, but always with borrowed weapons. I knew that there was no way I could continue to shoot competitively as well as go rallying, and stalking was something one could do from time to time. These deals complete, it was time to pack my small but carefully selected theological library, my teapot and electric coffee perculator, two decanters and some glasses and a small selection of pewter tankards, (pint size) and proceed to Wells Theological College.

Having already inadvertently missed a term I deemed it prudent to arrive a couple of days early for this term. I had arranged for an interview with the Principal, Canon Howarth, and my landlady agreed to have my room ready.

Wells, when it is not full of tourists, is a beautiful and fascinating place surrounded by Mendip myth and legend and such places as Wookey Hole. The college consisted of a building adjacent to the Cathedral in which were a library and lecture room and sort of common room. Students were housed in various cottages in Vicar's Close and catered for by a variety of landladies, some more enterprising than others. We used the Cathedral Lady chapel for our corporate worship and there was a small chapel at the top of the close for voluntary services, meditation and so on. There was a reasonable selection of decent drinking houses, 'The Swan' being highly commended, but it didn't suit me. 'The Crown' became my spiritual home, the back bar run with tremendous efficiency and glee by

Peggy, and 'The White Harte' was a good second. There was also 'The Fountain', adjacent to our digs where they were quite happy to fill one of our lovely large wash water jugs (plumbing was primitive in Vicars Close) with draught scrumpy, which helped to wash down the attempts at food of Mrs. James our good landlady. I have never known anyone else who could produce day after day two or three courses of stodge, pastry and potatoes predominated in her culinery closet. I mentioned earlier that Wells took older men. In our house apart from three of us all ex-National Service and ex-Cambridge, we had an ex-Naval Commander, the ex-head of CID in Burma, and a retired Brigadier, Hugh Stubbs, retired Brigadier was perhaps the most explosive over food. After two hours or more of extremely cold ecclesiastical exercises Mrs. James produced for Sunday breakfast one pullets egg per person, with the usual mountains of soggy white bread. Hugh regarded this meagre offering, "Boiled egg, Mrs. James, boiled egg is a tea dish". And he did not mean Lancashire Yorkshire type tea with ham and chips, but tea afternoon, with sandwiches cucumber, where a pullets egg might well have been acceptable. It is hard to make one sardine, split down the middle, cover a complete piece of toast, but Mrs. James could do it. We used a lot of Heinz mayonnaise which we imported and copious quantities of scrumpy in order to survive.

My interview with Canon Howarth was very good. He asked all about rallies and my part, and agreed that while I should make best use of my time when at college, I should take every drive I was offered. We had a conversation a few months later when I came back from a successful outing during which he intimated that while Minis were acceptable in Vicars Close, works Healeys were not, and please would I find somewhere else to park these when I had one about me. The college, he reminded me, existed to promote "the quiet life" and the Healey exhaust note, while no doubt music to some, did not really contribute to this promotional ideal.

The two other Cambridge men were Maurice Bartlett, now in charge at Lancaster Priory and Philip Morgan, presently a Canon in Watford. The team was made up by one other late starter, Michael Walls, who, although born in England was brought up in Johannesberg where his father was Archdeacon. Mike had graduated at Capetown. Mike later married the elder of my two sisters and both he and Maurice were to conduct our wedding in the course of time. Philip co-drove for me on two Monte Carlo rallies, both of which we finished. Our day started with meditation either in the Close Chapel or in the Cathedral, although I think a few meditated in bed. I have never had any trouble getting up and took tea to Mike and Philip at 6.30 and then meditated in the Cloisters, sometimes very cold and damp but nearly always peaceful and rarely visited by anyone else.

Morning Prayer followed at 7.30 and Communion at 8 am, then Mrs. James' attempt at breakfast. An office was said just before luncheon and it was sometimes a rush to return from 'The Crown' in time for this. Attendance at Evensong was also supposed to be compulsory but if one was delayed duck shooting, tickling trout or poaching pheasant the Principal would pardon upon receipt of a small portion of the "produce" of our labours. My programme was such that I had ample time to pop over to Cambridge and encourage the CUAC lads, and sup some ale. I then usually slept a while setting out in time to return for meditation. I was also called to Abingdon to confer with Marcus. Monte plans were afoot.

The Mini had been announced and Marcus himself had driven one on the Viking, and some were also entered in the Portuguese and the RAC as a trial outing. It was felt that the superb roadholding would, at least to some degree, compensate for the lack of power and Marcus decided, partly to please the publicity boys, to enter six Minis, three to start from Paris, three from Oslo. There was also an A40 for Pat and Ann. I was to go with Peter again and start from Oslo. It was hoped that some time after Christmas we would all have an outing in a Mini on a commercial skid pan in the Midlands. I returned to college, heart on high, only to witness a rather tedious Christmas performance put on mostly by second year students. The worst feature of an indifferent evening was that it finished after closing time. However, the good Peggy had kept the back bar open. It was about this time that we formed a college skittle team. This excellent game was played in special alleys behind pubs, usually involving a lovely log fire and a bar dispensing only scrumpy. We played in many a Mendip pub without expertise but displaying a good thirst, always suitably assuaged by the end of the evening. Meditation after skittles was sometimes somewhat blurred.

On my way home for Christmas I had a navigational conference with Peter. Working together for the second time made things much easier and I soon had a fair grip of what was required. At home we did a great deal of beagling (I needed the exercise, no longer having the facility to play squash) and helped out with Christmas at our Parish church, but was glad that when the festivities were over, the call came to attend the skid pan. Robbie Slotemaker came to instruct us and I think what struck all of us initially was how incredibly small the actual skid pan was, until Robbie demonstrated how to use the space. A selection of Minis was available and those who had not yet driven one were allowed a few minutes on the roads adjoining the pan. We were given a talk about weight transfer and cadance braking, and flicking the wheel right before a leftwards twiddle. Then he demonstrated a 180° spin, useful when observing a police road block ahead or on being conscious of an accident approaching and preferring to meet it tail first rather than head first. We then all learned to do it, some with more success than others, as is normally the case. Robbie then demonstrated the 360° which, as far as I could see, served no useful purpose at all, but was quite a jolly thing to be able to do. Essentially it all taught car control in slippery situation (such as a police blockade) and an additional use of the handbrake and so on. I felt that cadance braking was just a fancy name for something most of us already practised. However it was good to get together, meet some other team members and have an introduction to a Mini, in which, in various guises I was to do so many miles on the road and in competition.

Peter collected me from home to go and embark at Newcastle for the sail to Oslo, and let me drive some of the way to get to know the motor. We met up in Newcastle with Pat and Ann who had arrived in good time. Other team members and some Rootes group entries were also in town. Marcus telephoned from Paris to say that we would be required to attend a reception at the British Embassy in Oslo and please be properly dressed. At that time I only owned one suit and that, in anticipation of a finish, was on its way to Monte Carlo in a Castrol van. Castrol frequently ran this sort of service for crews who wanted some decent gear at the finish but did not want extra weight in the car. In one's Bentley or Jaguar one may as well use the matching suitcases, in an 850 cc Mini weight and space were at a premium, although there was more space than in a Healey.

Pat and Ann immediately volunteered to take "The Bishop" shopping in the morning to buy a suit in the January sales. This was a memorable expedition which caused hysteria in a number of gents' outfitters, but eventually for seven pounds and ten shillings matching top and bottom in a blue-grey colour were selected as being ideal for an embassy visit. We made our way to the docks and the ferry.

In splitting the team Marcus was guarding against a total disaster. Each year that I can remember in those days and earlier, according to records there has always been one starting point from which no competitors got through, or that only a few made it and that with great loss of penalties. Athens was so dicey that at one point entries got bonus points for attempting it. Even without snow in northern Greece and Yugoslavia, roads were bad and garages almost non-existent. Quite often those entries never got out of Yugoslavia in time to finish. Sometimes the Lisbon people came to a full stop in the Pyrenees, sometimes snow in the Ardennes hit Paris, Frankfurt and Scandinavian starters. The Glasgow folk had to make the cross-Channel boat, and even the Monte Carlo starters could have trouble during their first go at the Alps or in Alsace or the Ardennes, and so on. So it made sense to split the team.

In the days before the Second World War reaching Monte Carlo was the only goal. My uncle Joe set out from Warsaw in a Lancia,

Les Leston and Peter Jopp in Rootes team Rapier shortly after leaving Oslo. We had snow nearly all the way, but it was the first year that studded tyres were generally available to works teams.

became completely snowbound, eventually got a traon to Paris and drove the rest of the way to arrive two days late, but to arrive. The organisers awarded them a special trophy. We hoped that our trip would be a little less dramatic and anyhow with different starting points being used, some of us ought to arrive.

Also on the boat were Tish Ozanne and Pat Allison (Mini) and Nancy Mitchell, European Ladies Champion in 1956 and 1957. From Rootes, team manager Norman Garrard was accompanied by Rosemary Smith, Paddy Hopkirk, Peter Jopp and Les Leston. Joppy proudly showed off a lovely new watch. Norman Garrard set up in the saloon and organised games, others took advantage of the various facilities. Before we docked Joppy revealed that his "new watch" was the receiver for a miniature tape recorder, and where he had not been, with the wretched thing in action, was nobody's business. To a young theological student it was mildly educational and hearing the tape played during our last breakfast on board produced some rather red faces.

The visit to the embassy was a great success, Les Leston making a superb speech, extremely funny, but in no way disrespectful and certainly calculated to make officials think quite highly of us curious horseless carriage conductors. I was able to use my new suit again next day when several of the BMC team accompanied me to the Anglican chapel for Sunday morning service. Some members of the Rootes team poured on a little mild scorn and suggested that we were going to pray to win. I said no, "only to do our best". I had never been to Scandinavia before so we had an all too brief look at Oslo and also talked to a number of Norwegians. The Norwegian war record I had studied and had come rather to admire them as a nation. All too soon it was time to start. There was a little snow in Oslo and as we had, I think for the first time, the availability of studded tyres, we used them. They were Dunlop Durabands with tungsten tipped studs laboriously screwed in by hand, and on a dry road one sounded like a little tank. But they were well put together and Peter and I ran on the same set right through to Monte in spite of quite a lot of Tarmac. Leaving Norway for Sweden we changed back to driving on the left and then after the short ferry trip to Copenhagen it was right hand side again. Denmark had a low speed limit, strictly enforced, and as there was nothing on the roads life became rather exasperating as we were experiencing a problem and yet could not build up much time to deal with it. The problem was icing in the carburettor caused by very cold mist. Eventually we made a tube or duct out of an empty Carlsberg can to duct warm air from manifold to carburettor. Future Minis were modified to

"to complete the road section and my first trip to Monte". Note the early studs and Rupert has started to grow a beard. We have arrived in Monte Carlo.

avoid this problem, perhaps at least in part due to our experience. We ran down to Frankfurt and then back to the Ardennes where any boredom ended abruptly. Previous heavy falls of snow were being supplemented by a small blizzard. A car ahead was stationary but I persuaded Pete to charge into the deep snow at one side to try to pass it. This proved entirely successful, the Mini grappling with its studded little front wheels to whoosh us through the deep and back on track. We were greatly encouraged and made the next control with a few minutes in hand when many others were late. Now we turned south towards Grenoble, Chambery and the real rally. We rejoiced, Minis could do it, much more than a motorised roller skate and potentially a real rally car. Hitting the "common route" and serious rallying we began to get news from other starting points and some had had a really rough ride. We were on packed snow or ice most of the rest of the way to Monte, studs serving us well, and my Michelin map navigation had improved.

A few kilometres out of Monte the snow left off and our "little tank" trundled down various corniche to the gas works hairpin (yes, even Monte has a gas works) and on to the Promenade to complete the road section and my first trip to Monte. We got a great welcome and went to eat, sleep and prepare for the mountain circuit.

This was transition period for the Monte. The long drag from a far distant starting point or a circuituous route around Europe was no longer test enough, and although the mountain circuit already existed after arrival, as well as the dash round the grand prix circuit,

"The Morleys were soon losing water ... we were able to help on the odd occasion". Rupert and Don book in and Peter offers our water supply. Mountain circuit, note the studs again.

this was not enough. In the year in question, 1960, the challenge from the works Mercs, after weeks of practice was almost certain to prove successful as indeed it did, with a 1, 2, 3 victory. The following year a curious form of handicap was involved. On this year one had to make some sort of attempt to do, as near as possible, the same time on each section of two laps of the mountain circuit. Ann Wisdom thoroughly appreciated what was needed with the result that she and Pat did very well, coming seventeenth overall and winning the ladies award. Of the Minis, Tish and Nancy were already out and Alec Pitts car was badly battered and tied up with string after an altercation with a milk float, (I didn't know the French had them) and finished 73rd overall. Three crews however were still going well. Tommy Wisdom and Jack Hay, Donald and Erle Morley and Peter and I. The Morleys started the mountain circuit ahead of us, Tommy was some way behind, crews starting in their rally order, but the Morleys were soon losing water. We were able to help them on the odd occasion, but they were losing time as well. I am not sure that I really understood the timing arrangements, but Peter was fast and consistent and this super performance took us up a place or two and we finished 23rd. I believe this to be the highest placing ever for a standard 850 cc Mini. After the rally was over I wanted to get back home and miss the razzamatazz and Peter was not bothered, so we set out at about mid-day to get up into the mountains. We found a delightful pub with a good menu, where we were joined by Alex Pitts and Tony Ambrose. Marcus had said that I might keep the car for the Cambridge Mini Monte rally, so I was

"... Peter was fast and consistent and this super performance took us up a place or two and we finished 23rd..." Bear battling well.

able to take it home and later to Wells. So the meal we had that night really set the seal on my first Monte, a good finish, a first for the Mini, the car to go home in and discussions with Marcus in two or three weeks time about the rest of the year.

The organisation and efficiency of the "works Mercs team" was almost beyond belief, but the cost must have been quite stupendous compared with the budget Marcus had to play with. If memory serves correctly I think it was suggested that six Minis and an A40 on the Monte that year cost about £10,000. I cannot imagine that the Mercedes exercise was a mark less than ten times that amount. They got excellent publicity for their success, but Pat's achievement in winning the Ladies was also well covered and the Minis were talked about, photographed and written up everywhere. I sometimes think that Marcus got the better value for his money. It was quite a snowy year which was a good introduction for me, I was later to encounter an almost "dry" year and one which was just about "max snow".

My faults as a navigator were, no doubt, numerous. I was not much use at very detailed games with times, as on the mountain circuit,

Peter and Rupert about to start the mountain circuit, Rupert clearly showing his confusion with the timing arrangements, Peter just looking forward to the drive. I don't think I was really ever made to be a navigator except as far as maps are concerned. Complicated timing was a mystery to me and an unneccesary encumbrance.

and although my map reading was perhaps above average, I was far too often watching the road and the driver and deciding how I would do it. Going with Peter was glorious because he did things just like I thought I would do them, I was to have a few far less happy experiences.

David Hiam (Dunlop's man) came with me on the Mini Monte. The forecast was dreadful, heavy rain in Yorkshire and snow in the Lakes. We reckoned that we only had two serious opponents. I forget who, and the ex-Monte Mini was much admired. Although we led in the early stages we had to be satisfied with second in the end, as I am a pig-headed and stiff-necked "Bishop". The pre-supper section went well and we left Ilkley in high spirits only to have the exhaust fracture, so that we became a very noisy Mini, and the rains set in monsoon-like. We approached Dent village, a black spot, to be warned that the back road behind the village was a raging torrent and impassible. I refused to drive my noisy mini through the village and expressed grave doubts about the suggestion that the back road was "not on". Even going very slowly on a lot of revs, the water washed over the bonnet and the car kept trying to lift and go with the current. We got into the shallows at the far side before I let the light go out and we opened the door to push, allowing the water to flow right through the car, so that everything on the floor was soaked. On dry land David dried out the motor and we did the next few miles with the passenger door open on right handers to get water out of the office. The next car on the back road was an MGA which was washed into an adjoining field. We had lost ten minutes and were very lucky not to be similarly aquatically agriculturalised.

Later we successfully stormed Hard Knott heading east, in thick snow, only to be advised in Wrynose bottom that Wrynose was snowed up and that we should turn right and go round. The "Bishop" in his foolishness declared "ex cathedra" (from his driving seat) that if Hard Knott was on so was Wrynose. It wasn't. We wasted half an hour, but very few people were still in and of that few we were second. We had of course the advantage of studs (although rather worn) which the others did not. David later rewarded me by taking me twice to navigate for him on The Welsh, once in his faithful Minor 1000 and once in his Mini.

And so back to Wells, theology, golf with Brigadier Stubbs, skittles and scrumpy in Peggy's back bar at the Crown. The cloisters were cold for meditation in January and February.

"Of towing and Tulips, Trollhatten and Alpine Trials"

The Monte Mini caused quite a stir in college and Wells generally, all sorts of people wanting a ride in it. The Mendip roads were quiet at that time of year so some people, a carefully selected few, were taken out for "quick" runs, Cheddar Gorge down hill being one of the favourites. When I returned her to Abingdon, Marcus agreed that I should not miss any more college until after Easter, but he had quite a full summer mapped out for me, providing the Principal agreed. My Thames van seemed a bit pedestrian and faceless after the Mini; but it took me back to Wells, and many miles after that. The Principal did agree, so I really got on with college life and with preparations for Easter, both in college and Cathedral. As a total contrast to rallying the peace and quiet of our college lives was curiously stimulating. Apart from regular times for drinkies I played some golf with Brigadier Stubbs, Hugh and I being just about equally bad at this most frustrating of games and some of the senior officers language, loud and clear across coomb and vale, was more that of an army commander in the midst of battle than of a theological student purposefully pursuing a little white ball. I did a little duck shooting and made the odd expedition to the farm of my uncle and aunt on the edge of Dartmoor. I took some nights off for the occasional rally, and also embarked on some serious testing of various "wakey" pills, trying to simulate the Liege, in terms of hours, by driving during the night (a succession of test cars seemed to come my way about this time) and doing college work during the day. The fourth days work was rarely satisfactory, but the tests proved useful.

I think it was about this time that I was involved in the first of three long distance towing exercises. Arthur and the Hurg had come across a lamp post which, most disagreeably, refused to get out of the way. The lamp post apparently stood firm and A & H stopped abreast of it. Upon looking upwards (for whatever purpose) Arthur observed the lamp post to be insecure and definitely undecided about what steps it should take. He abandoned the Hurg as the lamp post, ever so slowly toppled over. Arthur assured me that the corporation charge an inordinate amount to replace such concrete monoliths. For reasons totally obscure to me the engine of the Hurg was to be re-built in East Anglia and the rest of it in Birmingham. Time came for mating, and who better to sit at the wheel of an engine-less motor on a cold, foggy, freezing, muddy, dirty day than an underemployed theological student? I have done some lousy winter runs on bikes, but that was about the lousiest motoring experience in my book. Windscreen wipers couldn't work, through lack of a power source, so it was windscreen flat. Headgear I had, goggles I had not. Muck and mud froze to my face, seeing out of my half frozen-up eyes to brake, was a nightmare, and as darkness was coming at us time was of the essence. Some kindly soul at Cambridge stood by with soup and brandy which we willingly and thankfully took on board before going off again into the mist, murk, mud and gloom of East Anglia.

We arrived, and the good harbourer of the Hurg engine, proceeded from the door of his beautiful house and took one look at me, and said "A bath, sir and whisky, rum or brandy?" I opted for brandy, was helped to unpeel and sank into the foaming hot water. We were back in Cambridge in Arthur's A55 in good time for a pint at the 'Bath' and fillet steak and a fried egg at the adjacent restaurant. As so often in "situations" I think we stayed at Jay Scott Browns that night, not lingering over our steaks but returned thither and in good

"...our brakes provided considerable excitement ... because they frequently failed to fulfil their function". Proved by the bent panels front and rear.

time to enjoy her superb hospitality and excellent coffee and to give news of various chums. Later on I was to be towed from somewhere near Cambridge to Bolton in Lancashire in a veteran car which John Clarke had purchased, this in some way repaid his generousity in allowing me to drive his cars in various speed trials. This trip had its moments, but was nothing like so vicious. Some years later we were to tow a Cooper 'S' from Brasov in Rumania to Vienna, after a rally failure and the mechanics then had to get it back to Rochdale, but in Vienna a fixed tow was obtained, while Tony Fall and I flew home, but that one is another story.

My next international outing was the Tulip, as co-driver to Ken James in a Mini. To those who did well in the Tulip I mean no disrespect, but I had never regarded it as a serious rally. It seemed to me to consume a lot of miles for a very small number of special tests, timed passes and hill climbs. Minis were still having teething troubles, and ours consistently suffered petrol pump failure, this essential element at that time being housed in the dirty, dusty, muddy recesses of the rear wheel arch or what used to be mudguard. Also our brakes provided considerable excitement, being some early discs in preparation for the Cooper, exciting because they frequently failed to fulfil their function. So it was not a happy outing. Added to this, although I got on well with Ken, I felt that I could certainly have driven as fast.

We saw some wonderful scenery, as the event went right down to Monte and used the Col d'Turini. We met lots of pals and we

"We saw some wonderful scenery ... but more than that I cannot say". Ken and Rupert in action.

finished, but more than that I cannot say. And I still feel that the Tulip was a series of driving tests connected by long and very boring road sections. I reported to Marcus. His reaction was, well you get the drive on the Alpine, but you must take Ken as co-driver. Ken was not keen, feeling that it was his fault that he and John Gott had wrong slotted on the Liege, and quite frankly not seeing himself as a navigator. However that story comes later. Before the Alpine I was paired with Peter again, to do something which even now seems most unlikely. Marcus wanted us to take a Wolseley 6/99 to Sweden to compete in the Midnight Sun Rally. The reason for this was that quite a few Wolseleys were sold in Sweden and the dealers had asked for an entry. The car was fitted with a full Healey engine and a central change gearbox (instead of steering column change). Marcus wanted the car in Marseilles as a spare service car for the Alpine, some week or ten days after the finish of the Swedish outing, and asked me if I would like to drive it down, having a look at some of the Alpine route on the way. It was going to be a rush to get to Stockholm in time, but after that I had no special plans, so that seemed to fit together quite well. I had examinations to take in Wells amost up to the start of the rally so Marcus arranged a flight for me. I came out of my last exam about an hour early, having written dangerously fast for the first two hours, urged the Thames to Abingdon as fast as she would go, abandoned her, to be driven on to Heathrow by Douggie Hamblin in a Healey and making the flight no more than conveniently. The flight went via Copenhagen and so it was towards dinner time when we made Stockholm where Peter met me and took me via a round about route to see the waterfront and other sights while there was still time, to our base. At our hotel Pat and Ann were waiting for us so that we could dine together. I had been asked by Peter Garnier of 'Autocar' to write up the event for them and to take some photos and as a result the following copy appeared in the issue out the week after the event.

Locals Win Rally of the Midnight Sun

Ostersund, Saturday, 18th June

This is one of the events in the International Calendar in which the Scandinavians have the opportunity to show other rally drivers of Europe how to deal with their particular type of gravel road. That people who are born and bred to this type of motoring should be better at it than the rest who were brought up on tarmac is not surprising, but few realize how much the rest still have to learn. They are gravel roads of a very high standard, upon which cruising speeds of over 80 m.p.h., and maximum speeds of over 100 m.p.h., are not difficult to attain, and the dust does not seem so

Pre-rally conference. Peter Riley, Ann Wisdom as she was, now married to Peter, Erik Carlsson and Pat Moss, now married to Erik.

thick and penetrating as that of Yugoslavia and East Africa. Most British rally drivers have no conception of the sort of driving required to appear in the awards list of the Midnight Sun.

British entry for the event was not large. There were five locally entered Ford Anglias and four Sunbeam Rapiers, and four more Anglias driven by Jeff Uren and Fergus Sayer, Vic Preston and Sam Croft-Pearson, Dacre-Lacy and Douglas Wright, and Anne Hall and Valerie Domleo. The Austin A40 driven by Patt Moss and Ann Wisdom, and a Wolseley 6/99 driven by Peter Riley and Rupert Jones, made up the total British contingent.

This year's event started in Stockholm on the morning of Wednesday, 15 June. First car to leave the starting ramp at 8 a.m. was an ID Citroen, followed by a Chevrolet Corvair and then by four Mercedes. The last of these was to have been driven by Shock and Moll, but they did not appear because of illness, and this car was given to Bohringer and Socher.

The route was in two loops, the more southerly one first. Drivers returned almost to Stockholm before heading north to the bleak, rolling country not far south of the Arctic Circle, and then a little way south to the lakeside town of Ostersund, and the finish. The road sections were relatively easy in that averages were not high, but the navigation needed fairly constant work, and driving almost entirely on gravel roads becomes tiring. Only one road section exceeded 200 km in length so never was it possible to make up much more than half an hour for rest and refreshment, and at the end of each section was a special stage or special test. So from 8 a.m. Wednesday until 4 p.m. Friday crews worked fairly hard.

Special stages were sections of closed road from 5km to 30km in length, for which either a very high average was set or the fastest time recorded in each class became the standard time for that class. Marks lost on the road section were of small importance, since one minute late on the road was the equivalent of 5 sec in a special stage. The driving tests were intended as tie deciders, but although they were in many respects similar to British special tests, there was one essential difference — they were all very long.

Leaving Stockholm, the convoy travelled west on a main road route and then into the country, to arrive at Arbod for the first test, consisting of 1 ½ km round the back streets of the town, part gravel part tarmac, including four chicanes and two stop astride lines.

Two Saabs had the misfortune to turn over on this test, at the point where competitors went from gravel to tarmac. From this it might be supposed that the casualty rate was high, but something like 80 per cent of the starters were also finishers and the Saab of Bromark which turned over here finished second in the class. The crew worked very hard in every spare minute available, and by the time they reached the finish all the dents had been beaten out or filled.

After completing the first of many winding, switchback special stages, competitors arrived at the small race track near Karlskoga for the second test, in which four cars started at once and did two laps — one standing, one flying.

Vic Preston, trying his hand at some Swedish gravel instead of that of his native East Africa, had engine trouble here with his Anglia, but was able to get going again. Pat Moss went considerably faster than Anne Hall, but farther back in the field Ewy Rosquist in her Volvo was a hot favourite for the Ladies' Award. The works Mercedes of Bohringer went very well, but in the big class the surprise was the 2,100 Fiat of Erik Berger which was putting up excellent times and being brilliantly driven, especially on gravel.

The next test was a hill-climb near Jönköping, where there was some delay as competitors had to return to the bottom in groups, but as coffee was avavilable at the top this did not matter much. The unfortunate Preston again had trouble here, with the distri-

distributor cap flying off halfway up the hill. At this time competitors were faced with about 2½ hour of semi-darkness — the only time headlamps were used throughout the event.

A long special stage followed, the early numbers getting a good deal of early morning mist. The sun was up soon after 3 a.m. and the route led back towards Stockholm via two more special stages. Before reaching Stockholm the route led north on to the second leg.

Pattern of the results was beginning to take its form. Among the big saloons, Bohringer in the Mercedes was being beaten by the amazing Berger in his Fiat, and Bohringer was heard to admit that he had never tried so hard before. Carl-Magnus Skogh in a standard Saab was putting up almost unbelievable times in one special stage after another, often beating the modified Saabs. The two Gunnars, Andersson and Callbo, were having a bit of a battle in the modified class with their Volvos, with Andersson gradually taking the lead. In the standard Volvo class Hans Ingier from Norway was hard on the heels of Rolf Carlsson from Stockholm.

On the first special stage of the northern leg near Upsala, Claudine Vanson and Renée Wagner lost their ID Citroen and

The Wolseley awaiting a stage.

departed into the rockery; they were both unhurt but the car was too badly damaged to continue. The corner was indeed a nasty one, and René Trautmann admitted having had quite a moment there in his Citroen. Farther on in the same section, the Bohringer Mercedes came to grief trying too hard to catch the flying Berger in his Fiat; the Mercedes went off on a very fast stretch and could just be seen hiding in the bulrushes well off the road.

So the relentless round continued well into the second day, working up the coast via Gaule and Sundsvall to Sollefta, never more than 200km passing without a few kilometres of closed road, and racing speeds over blind bumps followed by right-angle bends. The weather was really glorious, and as competitors started each stage at the minute intervals they were not much affected by the dust trails of other cars.

At Sollefta came the first offical stop of one hour and an excellent dinner was laid on. The Rally was now split in two, for a lady living along one of the special stages had elected to have a baby during the event, and all later numbers were held up for an hour. This was shortly after midnight — and it was still quite light enough to take photographs. Side lamps were not necessary for driving, and navigation without lights was quite possible. By 1.30 a.m. dawn was evident and soon after 2 a.m. the sun was making driving without sunglasses quite a problem.

At Vilhelmina there was a further 45min break for coffee; shortly after this Callbo's co-driver crashed their Volvo and Callbo broke

Pat and Ann in action in the A40.

his shoulder. However, they put the car back on its wheels and pressed on to the finish, and second place in the class behind Andersson.

A hill-climb on a loose surface which followed cost a Thunderbird its exhaust system on one of the very tight hairpins. Two more special stages took the competitors to Ostersund; on the first of these Erik Carlsson lost the Saab at nearly 100 m.p.h., narrowly missing the crowds of spectators, and went into the woods at a great speed. However,he and his co-driver appeared at dinner that evening completely unharmed. The Saab had finished up by snapping a telegraph pole in half nearly 150yd from where the accident began.

A final test was held on arrival at Ostersund and the results were produced very quickly indeed. In fact, the organization of the event was excellent throughout.

Skogh's winning drive in a standard Saab was a great achievement; Harry Bengtsson was quite a long way behind in his Porsche. Ewy Rosquist won the Ladies' Award, very closely challenged by Anne Hall, who drove very well to come so close to Ewy on her own ground; Pat Moss was third. So the Rally of the Midnight Sun ended, as it had begun, in brilliant sunshine. *R.S.L.J.*

RESULTS

General Classification: 1. Saab 96 (C. Skogh). 129 marks; 2. Porsche Super 90 (H. Bengtsson), 156; 3 Volvo 544 (G. Andersson). 194; 4. Volvo (R. Carlsson). 201; 5. Volvo 544 (H. Ingier),232; 6. Volkswagen (B. Söderström), 238; 7. Fiat 2,100 (E. Berger), 255; 8. Volswagen (B. Jansson), 262; 9. Volkswagen (R. Larsson), 296; 10. Auto-Union 1000 (H. Carlsson), 299; 11. Volkswagen (H. Källström), 307; 12. Volvo (K. Olofsson),311.

Ladies Award: 1. Volvo 544 (Ewy Rosquist),656; 2. Ford Anglia (Anne Hall), 675; 3. Austin A.40 (P. Moss) 780.

Team Award: 1. Volkswagen (H. Källström, B. Jansson and R. Larson)), 865; 2. Volvo (G. Callbo. G. Andersson and H. Ingier),941; 3. DKW (F. Olsson, S. Gilimo and O. Matti), 1,897.

After we had finished Pete and I went with Erik to where he had crashed to try and make his car safe and remove valuables until such time as Saab recovery arrived. As we got to the vehicle a small crowd watched a man freeing the battery with a view no doubt to stealing it. Erik, the big man, stood behind him until he had finished, then taking the battery from him said "Thank you, you have saved me work". The man melted into the forest, and we removed all other moveable goodies.

It should perhaps be added that Pat complained that the A40 was down on power and when it got back to Abingdon it was discovered that the cylinder block was cracked. It also seemed to me, about this time and purely as a casual observer, but perhaps with an eye to future business, that Pat Moss and Erik Carlsson seemed to be seeing quite a lot of each other, and that Peter Riley and Ann Wisdom chatted happily together when opportunity arose.

After an excellent reception and prize giving our little contingent returned to Stockholm where Pat, Ann and Peter were put on a flight back home. Brian Moylan, one of the works mechanics was to drive to Gothenberg in the A40 and take a boat back to England. Erik, having heard that I was driving south said that so was he and that we should travel together and I was to report to the SAAB works at Trollhotten and meet him. He and his co-driver, with car, were going by train from Hamburg to Basel and then practising for the Alpine. I queried whether Marcus would stand the train fare but the general opinion was that he would, so I agreed. I followed Brian in the limping A40 until our routes separated and then reported to SAAB's. Erik gave me a great welcome and a guided tour of the factory, followed by a very adequate drink when we arrived at my hotel. He called for me later and we went for a flight around the area in a small SAAB plane which was interesting, and a new experience for me as, at that time, I had never been up in a small aircraft. The pilot, as well as showing us the countryside, town and factory, threw the machine around a bit, but I was not put off, Erik was obviously valued at work and it seemed unlikely that anything unexpected would happen. We spent a very liquid evening, interrupted by some excellent food and then Erik announced that I should pay my bill as he would be outside at 4 am and he expected me to be in the Wolseley with all cylinders firing at that time. There was no trouble with the cylinders, it was my eyes, which in spite of repeated washing, were not keen to absorb either the delights of the Swedish landscape or the perils of the highway. Most inconvenient and thoughtless of them, and I cannot really think what the protest was about, I mean, a quiet evening with Erik, oh well, where was Marseilles? Whoops, was that Gothenburg? Perhaps a cigar might help? It did, and soon we were at Varberg station where we met Erik's co-driver Walther, and set off again at high speed.

Life was definitely for living again and at the station I mentioned breakfast to Erik to which he replied "No, Bishop, you wait, we eat later". We swept on to the ferry for Copenhagen, I hopefully thinking of some well known haunt of Erik's where food might occur. Hopes were dashed, Copenhagen left behind and Erik pounding on in front, taking only scant notice of Danish speed limits. At Gedser we stopped at a ferry terminal and Erik announced "Very soon we eat, Bishop". We boarded for three hour crossing to Travemunde, and paid the equivalent of ten shillings, sorry fifty pence, on entering the restaurant. There was the most incredible display of food, both hot and cold and Erik explained that for our entrance fee we could eat as much as we wanted during the crossing. I began to see why the big man had been prepared to abstain until now. The shipping company can have made little profit on Erik, and his speed accident of three days ago had not affected his appetite. On the same ferry were the Volvo team, three rally cars and a "service" estate, and we were all heading for the train at Hamburg. We were a little pushed for time. Erik knew the way and elected to lead followed by four Volvos and me. I did not know my way, did not know Hamburg or its Bahnhof , did not and do not like driving in strange cities, but did know, from army experience, that the last Johnny in a convoy is likely to have to drive twice as fast as the first. Add to this hazards such as traffic lights changing as the second Volvo went by at every junction, ensuring that Rupert repeatedly crossed on the "red", it was perhaps not surprising that the Polizei were showing an interest as this high speed cortege converged on the station. I say converged because we hit a "one way" system and the first two cars chose one direction and the other three another. We were dreadfully short of time and our "escort" seemed to have homed in on me. I stopped, I had one advantage, a slight knowledge of the German language. "Train to catch — Hamburg — Basel — international rally driver". "I understand" said the good officer, "Follow me". I did and two warehouses and a platform later the Wolseley was the first to be loaded on to the train.

The pace was beginning to tell and I foolishly hoped for a quiet night. I suppose we did use our very expensive bunks but Basel brought breakfast and a new day far too soon. Fresh mountain air, black coffee and the joy of prolonged pass bashing soon took over and we were well into the Alpine route when we stopped late for a picnic lunch. We worked on then, except for a supper stop, through the night until noon next day. We had a sandwich and agreed another section or so. I forget the col but we had a good climb up and I was desperately but hopelessly trying to hold Erik on the way down. The Wolseley's handling was quite superb and those big carbs pumped essence into the large combustion chambers producing a very satisfactory supply of smoothly available power. It was hot, I was sticky but happy, and in the knowledge that Erik was clearing the way, going very, very fast indeed. The BANG followed by lesser machine gun type reports almost caused deafness, but we pulled up in a straight line on the only straight piece of pass for kilometres. The Dunlop Duraband (an early form of radial tyre and not a golf or tennis toy) had done its thing. We knew about it on Healeys but I hadn't suspected either me or the Wolseley to get so excited. A third of the tread had found its spiritual home on this Alp and the remainder of the tyre, as they say in these parts of Lancashire where I write, had become "unpumped". Erik's little ring a ding ding two stroke SAAB sang happily on down the mountain side. The 'Bishop' bunged the jack in the orifice provided and started to wind up, having chocked the front wheels. It was really too hot for all this and it seemed days since alcoholic refreshment on the excellent train. Erik returned as I finished my labours, inspected the tortured tyre and decreed an end to practice. We turned towards the main road, a good pub, good food and bed. Tomorrow we could make Marseilles for late luncheon time. Erik knew a place to stay tonight. We drove to a pleasant auberge on the outskirts of Grenoble where we were given a superb welcome and shown to seats in the sun on a balcony. A head waiter in bow tie appeared as our host vanished towards the kitchen. "We drink beer, Bishop" said Erik. "Yes, Erik, please". "You are thirsty, Bishop? Walther and I are thirsty". Then turning to the excellent waiter Erik said "Ten beers please". "Ten beers?" queried the good man. "Yes Bishop is thirsty, French beer is not strong, we have ten beers each, thirty bottles, please". The evening pleasantly pursued its way.

BMC Competitions department had based itself at a delightful holiday resort La Ciotat, east of Marseilles and when I arrived one would not have thought that a major international rally was imminent, except in the area of Marcus Chambers domain. Most people seemed to be on the beach or in the ogin and totally relaxed. I couldn't relax at this stage. The Liege and the Alpine were the events I had dreamed of at my school desk along with the Mille Miglia and the Targa Florio. Events which were essentially motor races of a long distance kind. Man and machine would and should be really tested.

People used to say to me "Of course, you don't have to be really fit, like in other sports". Well, I have spent a lot of time on the squash courts, and I can say with confidence that a great deal of squash is no match for a 90 hour plus Liege, and three laps of the Targa Florio circuit are quite testing, especially when you know you have another three laps to do a little later.

It is almost incredible, but I have very rarely had the chance to drive a car before an international. This was my first international drive, I was quite determined to prove myself, and the only car that needed work doing on it when the team arrived was mine. It was really off the starting ramp that I first found my way around, and the first job was to fight our way out of Marseilles.

The little Mini seemed quite good. We had now some of the modifications which would make her a Cooper. The front discs were still as the Tulip car but with better linings, the proper central change was introduced and with a better syncromesh system on the gearbox and, if memory serves correctly, twin carburettors. We were number five and I think Erik number seven in the SAAB, certainly he was not far behind. The days of the HRG and the XK120 Jaguar had gone. Ian Appleyard, the first of only three winners of a Coupe d'Or or Gold Cup, in his famous Jaguar XK120 (registration NUB 120) was a memory and the organisers had made some changes. In the early days there was no outright winner of the Alpine, but anyone who completed the course and time trials (mostly well known passes) without penalty won a Coupe des Alpes and shared the prize money. Three successive penalty free outings won a Coupe d'Or, Stirling Moss drove a Sunbeam Talbot in 1952 and Alpines thereafter to win the second and John Venatier won the third on the last Alpine ever in 1970. But perhaps Appleyards effort was special, he used the same car on all three outings, had no works back-up and relied on his own organisation. Over the years through tedious Maths and Latin lessons I drove my school desk, perhaps with a concealed copy of 'Autocar' to help me ('Motoring News' was not born yet and 'Autosport' either very new or only embryo) up endless passes. I was Ian Appleyard, and I swept up Mont Ventoux, squirting all the power out of the Jaguar motor in a series of beautifully controlled drifts and slides round and out of those long exciting bends. I felt I knew the Col d'Allos as well as anyone, although I had never been there, and now it was off to Monza, where the Jaguar would have to work to hold the two remaining Ferraris. Then the route led back to France via the Vivionine and the Gavia; hello, why had some Italian peasant posted a high speed board rubber through the window into the office? "Jones, if you are with us, please decline the pluperfect of the verb "to love". There didn't seem to be much love about and "decline" described the present state of my academic career.

And now I was wending my way through the heavy traffic of Marseilles and out into the countryside. Our number was five, so many people were only just getting used to the idea that a rally was on the road but many junctions were manned by police and the pace soon hotted up.

Erik was only a couple of numbers behind me and soon came through and I tagged on behind. When we came to the first "selectif special" stage or whatever, a new game developed. Most of them were passes including both the up and down section. Erik, having to start two minutes behind me usually caught me somewhere near the summit, from my point of view, at or just over was ideal, then I latched on to him and got a very fast tow for a few kilometres until my nerve or my motor failed me and the SAAB ring a dinged off into the valley below. Erik could complete most "selectifs" with time to spare, so was waiting as I arrived, breathless and either late or nearly late. Erik cleared the crowds and in his best English announced, "Look out, Bishop comes", then he would grab the road book from us, get it stamped, pop it back through the window and

"Look out Bishop comes". Rupert in action.

wave us on our way. A lot of detail is lost in the mist of time, but at some point, I would think on day one, we arrived at the foot of Mont Ventoux, to attempt the famous climb. It was not Mini country, it was too fast and too steep and we enjoyed the scenery, and once again I dreamt of having power under the right hush puppy. The day would come but I have never yet been able to unleash it on that climb, perhaps one day, someone will lend me a suitable Ferrari, or again perhaps they won't? Although in many ways my dream car, I have never driven one, in spite of the odd offer. Pehaps I am afraid of being disappointed.

I was enjoying my Alpine and Ken was, with help, getting a grip of the navigation, and some long time after Ventoux we seemed to spurt off in the direction of Monza for some jolly motor racing. I made a great start in my race and was having a superb dice with I know not whom. So busy was I with the opposition that I totally neglected the marker boards for the hairpin and wondered why everyone else was slowing down. Off I went into some elephant grass over which I could not see, onto a grass banking....... from where I got an excellent view of all my colleagues disappearing towards the pits; we rejoined the ciruit a little behind the rest of the field.

O'Connor-Rorke in a Jaguar was fastest (was the engine a 'D' type?)

"I was enjoying my Alpine". I always enjoy running as an early number. The spectators are not yet bored and are thrilled to see you.

and Pat Moss a tremendous second in the Healey, with Don Morley equalling the Alpha time of Henri Oreiller who had also been fastest on Ventoux.

After Monza we tackled the Vivionne, fast up through the woods from the south side but very tight near the summit, with big drops, and all unsurfaced of course. Vivionne is one of the famous four passes in this area, the others the Croce Domini, very rough near the summit, the Gavia, smooth dirt, big drops, very, very fast in places, and I think my favourite and lastly the Stelvio, from Italy into Austria, which in this direction means fast side and tunnels first and forty nine lycets down the other side. It was at the control on the Austrian side, not on this event, that I first saw disc brakes glowing red through Borrani wire wheels after a very fast descent.

Back to the Alpine, and on the Vivionne, which I thoroughly enjoyed, Tommy Wisdom and Jack Hay in the Sprite came off and ended up with the front wheels over the edge of a deep drop. They abandoned ship, but by dint of jacking up the middle, Tommy was able to climb in again and reverse onto dry land.

Now started the long haul back to France with only one tight little

"Tommy Wisdom and Jack Hay in the Sprite" on the Vivionne shortly before their balancing act.

section to enliven things. But here Anne Hall elected to park her Ford Zephyr in an adjacent stream. When we went by she claimed to be alright apart from a cut on her hand, and said that her co-driver Val Domko had gone for help. We made Chamonix for a much needed overnight halt, but happy in the knowledge that we led our class from another Mini. The restart was mid-morning and we faced some thirty seven passes in twenty four hours of non-stop motoring. During the night an Italian entry overturned and caught fire. The first twenty cars had gone through before the route was closed because the forest was ablaze. After a long wait the rest of the entry, which included us, was sent back to Die and Parc Ferme, and again we waited. There is nothing more soul destroying or tiring than suddenly having all the hype removed and it is hard to wind up again. When we restarted again Ken and I were definitely jaded and in the hour before dawn, always a low time, we booked into a control four minutes early and incurred a big penalty. We no longer led the class as a result and I suggested to Ken as gently as possible that we look out for that mistake in future. Dawn came and with it sunshine and soon after, heat, which adversely affected tired minds and bodies. We were approaching the Col d'Allos, one of the greats, and Ken urged me on, we were going to be late. We slid to a stop by the control table and Ken jumped out and he returned with humble apologies, we had done it again, four minutes early. I said nothing but fury dwelt in my belly and I flung the little motor at the bloody Allos. We were going great guns, but two thirds up, a left and I was going too fast. We went up onto the grass, perhaps I could repeat the "Monza experience", but no, a rock blocked the passage of the near side front wheel. Unfortunately the rest of the motor continued for an inch or so causing some derangement at that end. I can never believe immediately that I am out of an event. I prevented Ken from de-bussing and reversed back onto the road and started to trundle upwards, frantically gripping the wheel to keep us pointing forwards. At a "passing point" I was persuaded to pull over and inspect the damage. We managed to bend things a little less crooked and ensure all was safe and started off again. Perhaps we might just finish in time. But there was no way and when we finally made Nice some two hours late my hands were dreadfully blistered. The hotel medico did things for my hands and the barman attended to my liquid requirements. Ken went to eat, I took a bottle of plonk to the bedroom and slept.

Waking in good time I observed a super day in terms of weather and a blue sea and sandy shore. Bedecked in bathers I crossed the promenade and was accosted by a French supporter of the Hitler Youth who invited me to pay a number of francs for the privilege of plunging into the ocean. Not being aware of the pay to plunge rules and not being in the habit of carrying a few thousand francs in my swimming trunks pocket, I returned to my room and wrathfully ruminated in a bath. Marcus joined me for breakfast when I was making up for not having eaten on the previous evening. None of your coffe and croissant for me on this occasion, having tackled fruit and fish I was into things of consequence like steak, chop, kidney and other goodies, and while in this department, why can't the French, superb in nearly all things culinary, fry eggs? Marcus listened to my tale of rallying woe, indicated that as everyone else had done well some jollification was in order at which I was welcome to join, but the Wolseley needed driving back to England and when I was ready to go, and only when I was ready would I like to take it, and return it to Abingdon in a couple of weeks? And, oh yes, he had thought of teaming me with John Gott on the Liege, how did I think about that? It was most kind of Marcus when I was rather low to pick things up in that way. It was also a great privilege to be asked to go with our team leader Chief Constable John Gott, and today as the chaplain to the Police in Rochdale I often think of the time that I was to spend with John with thankfulness and joy.

The days of professionalism were setting in and Peter Riley was to be teamed up with top navigator Tony Ambrose, both of whom had much more time for rallying than I would have in the near future as my clerical career began to develop. I enjoyed Nice and Eden Rock, some sort of millionaire's Butlins, for a few hours and thankfully climbed into my old Wolseley mate and headed for the mountains. I like mountains and mountain people. What was the name of that auberge in Serres?

The Liege of them all and the advent of Blessed Marigold

I had a really delightful drive back in the Wolseley and for a few weeks attempted an experience relatively rare to me. I had a go at it for some months between National Service and going "up" as they say, meaning starting Cambridge life. The experience is called "going to work". My uncle was company secretary at what was then the Gandy Belt Company in Wallasey which made a number of things from belts, both conveyor and drive, through to brake and clutch linings. My official title was "filing clerk" and I think I could add "failed" like maths and Latin, but when not thus engaged I found employment and enjoyment on the factory floor. I had added a motorcycle to my Thames van, as the cheapest way of getting to work, which had to be approached over various swing bridges through Birkenhead's then thriving dock land. The roads were criss-crossed with railway lines, very hazardous to the unwary motor-cyclist, and a swing bridge opening for a ship and unfavourable railway lines spelt disaster to one's time sheet. I took a little time out to watch Cambridge Racing in action, now managed by John Aley, but most of my thoughts were towards the Liege and towards my forthcoming ordination. I spent quite a lot of time helping at Neston Parish Church as we lived at Parkgate in that parish and also with my Royal Marine Reserve Unit, based not far from the Gandy Belt Company and involving those difficult railway lines again.

I suppose that during this time I was involved in my last rifle shooting competitions, mostly at Altcar ranges, where I had fired in my first serious competition from school at Rossall. I was glad to think that when I resigned from "The Corps" upon my ordination I would have an organised unit to visit regularly, the Borstal in the parish to which I was to go. I do like, to this day, at least a part of my life to be in a uniformed disciplined situation. At this time I also had a very unsatisfactory interview with the then Bishop of Chester, Gerald Ellison. It was unsatisfactory in that he thought highly of stalking and shooting but did not seem much interested in rallying, and seemed to feel that I might fit in well to some stockbroker belt parish, just the environment from which I was trying to escape. I saw my life differently, shooting in decline, rallying to continue on a limited basis and a parish in Lancashire

"so it left only the Stelvio, from the Austrian side". John Gott and Rupert in the 3,000 wait their time to attack the Stelvio's forty nine lycets.

out of Yugoslavia with a seven minute lead over Pat and Ann and Peter and Tony were well placed. David and Vic had several punctures and John and I more than our share. Also at speed the bonnet flew open and bent its little self and we had difficulty securing it again. John was suffering from heat and I had to drive some sections which were tight, but could not really enjoy them as I was worried about him. As the day cooled and we headed towards the passes Moistrocca and Predil and back to Italy he improved. We later learned that the Yugo section had dashed many hopes including two well placed Alfas and a Porsche. Sixty four cars went into Yugo but only twenty eight came out still in the rally. John and I were really glad to reach the first service point back in Italy at Tarvisio and David and Vic were fast moving up the field. Pat however, was in clutch trouble but still holding station just behind Peter and Tony. Now followed some very tight motoring in northern Italy during which several well placed cars went out, leaving the girls in the lead, the Sprinzel Sprite in an incredible second place and David and Vic and John and I still in the hunt. Peter and Tony went out when a fan blade came adrift and punctured the radiator.

"For most of the time it was unbearably hot and dusty ..." Much dustier than this picture taken in Yugoslavia shows.

Dawn came again and although we were still well placed John was not fit and I found myself both driving and navigating which went on all the rest of the way across Italy and into France. It was real work and the memory is hazy, but stupendous efforts were being made to sort out Pat's clutch problems and the team, apart from Peter, was still holding together. There was one very hard working night to go and then the long run back to Liege from Chambery.

John was totally against "wakey" pills, so respecting his view, I had left mine at home. I was still driving having been largely in sole charge for a lot of hours, including some of the Yugo section when we heard that Pat's clutch was sorted and this seemed to inspire John to come alive for the last night, which included about seven famous French passes. On the first, the "Allos" John drove well, on the next section we were competitive but on the Col de Luitel John drove brilliantly to make fastest time. Pat was third on that pass but still holding off the only real threat, that of the Porsche of the father and son Sanders. There were three more cols to go and we had a short break before we attempted them. We slept. John

"all the rest of the way across Italy and into France". Rupert tackles the Col du Larche as John rests. Note the bent bonnet.

had had quite a lot of sleep while not well, I had had none and no "wakeys". Somebody kindly woke us and I had to be lifted from the the drivers seat to the other side because I could not properly wake up and John had to set out without much support. It took me twenty minutes to really get back into gear. On "wakeys" that would never have happened. Judge for yourself, but of course it is irrelevant now as long rallies unbroken by nights in bed are no longer encouraged. The final three cols went without incident for us and the rest of the team. They were graft at the tail end of a long arduous event, but after the Luitel the result was in little doubt and most places were secure. The only person still really having to battle on was that incredible John Sprinzel gamely keeping the Sprite in touch with the Porsche. Rain came down heavily towards the final critical control at Chambery but it did not seem to matter, the battle was basically lost and won. At the Chambery control the three big Healeys needed nothing doing to them, the Sprite wanted a new wheel to replace a buckled one, about the only servicing it required in those three thousand miles which had devastated much more expensive tackle.

There was an incredible air of expectancy, something great about to be achieved, but it was only shortly after dawn and we still had a long run back to Liege, due to be reached about 4.30 pm.

It was Douggie Hamblin who had eventually cured Pat's clutch problems, which were as a result of a failed oil seal on the back of the gearbox. The right seal did not arrive in time but Douggie had the gearbox out, found a seal that would do in the garage they were using and had the box back and the show on the road again in under forty minutes. Ask your local garage for details. Pat left at high speed, cigarette in mouth and no doubt on "wakeys", but driving quite brilliantly, with Ann totally in command of timing and navigation. I think the really superb memories I have of those days, and the girls great success on this event perhaps highlight the very high degree of professionalism and competence from dedicated amateurs, and delightfully tempered with a sense of fun, good humour and comradeship, which existed. A mix which I shall never forget and I was highly privileged to be part of.

The rain didn't matter, we wandered around in it, our dust-covered clothing getting washed off, and then began to head for Liege. A short distance from Spa we found a convenient garage and washed the cars off. Those who had clean clothes changed into them and the girls powdered noses and so we headed for the finish. David

"Pat and Ann were first ... David and Vic ... fifth and John and I tenth". The victorious team at Spa before the Harley Davidson convoy into Liege. Dunlop's David Hiam had once again provided the "Bishop" with a suitable cigar, causing a severe fire risk.

Hiam, as usual now, appeared from somewhere with a large cigar for me, and so we finished. Pat and Ann were first, John Sprinzel third, David and Vic, a really super couple fifth, and John and I tenth. It was the most incredible result for the team, the first British car and crew to win this event, a first for the ladies, no ladies had won a championship event before and the first time that Great Britain had beaten all the other nations competing. About the only prize we had not won was that for the best French entered car. We had the Coupes des Dames, the Manufacturers Team Prize, the Club Team Prize and two class wins. The crowd in Spa seemed utterly delighted and again when we parked up in Liege after the usual high speed police Harley Davidson-directed convoy.

We went out to celebrate but we were clapped and people drifted off to bed quite soon. The prize giving was a succession of our team going up to collect pots. The girls looked quite superb and it was one of the highlights of my rallying career. John was now quite well and I was thrilled that I had been able to take the Healey wheel for so long on such an exacting event and prove that I could go well. It was interesting as well, as it confirmed my suspicions that I really preferred big powerful cars. I felt able to use the power and was in no way frightened to use it.

I dropped John off at his home in Northampton and with the permission of Marcus took the Healey back to Wells. I needed to try out some driving skills that I would not have used as a number two on a long distance event. I was never short of a passenger even at four in the morning, and a lot of rubber was left on the tarmac of Cheddar Gorge, but now I was quite sure that big hairy machines were within my capabilities. Money came through from bonuses and the Thames van was tired. In the local showroom I saw a Mini van, nearly within my financial grasp. Daddy was quite thrilled with the Liege result and I found the money to go north and take him out in the Healey, after which a slight financial top-up was forthcoming and I went back to Wells to clinch a deal on the Mini van, described as marigold in colour. That one had been sold, but a light green one was available tomorrow. She was beautiful and I called her Marigold. I could take delivery in two days and there was to be a break from college.

At very short notice I organised a trip to Scotland and took Mike Walls from South Africa with me. He had already been home with me and met the family. We made Cheshire for an evening meal and then drove through the night to Banff where a Cambridge friend and a member of Cambridge Racing royally entertained us at his parents' beautiful home. We arrived for breakfast, a good example of what a country house breakfast ought to be. We then went rough shooting, I with my Mauser rifle, Mike and John with shotguns. They took some birds and later I stalked and took a roe deer. We also bagged a hare, returning to base for luncheon. It was by now raining, so in the afternoon we "did" the distillery, including samples, by which time the weather and indeed everything else was pretty fine. John suggested "stooking". I was wearing quite well considering that I had driven all night, although Mike, who had slept in the back of the van a lot of the way was failing. We went out into nearby recently cut grain fields and hid ourselves in the piles of stooks, waiting for the birds coming in for evening food. Mike went to sleep and woke to find some large hairy horned Highland cattle looking into his hide and was somewhat concerned. We found him muttering something from the Psalms about "Fat bulls of Basan which fence me in from every side".

We headed south to Dumfries to stay a night or two with a Cambridge shooting friend at this delightful house. William Crawford is now a Queen's Counsel and while a very good shot, in terms of sport I think prefers fishing, but once again Mike and I were well looked after, and we enjoyed some shooting and it seemed to me that it was all part of his education. The Mini van was now going well, there is nothing like a lot of miles on a warm engine to complete the running-in process. Some time at my parents home was planned on the way south and it was not long after this visit that Mike became engaged to Su, the older of my two sisters. And so back to Wells via Dunlops, where I picked up some Durabands to replace the fairly inadequate standard rubber provided with the Mini.

Mike and I then worked very hard on a college Christmas production, a re-write of Gilbert and Sullivan's 'Trial by Jury', which was to be followed by a cabaret. This college jamboree was always attended by local Friends of the college and I think our efforts and those of many others were well rewarded when it was agreed by one and all to be one of the best ever. Just in case there are those who think theological colleges are essentially prudish places, the party continued well into the early morning in my room and others in Vicars Close with Peggy from the 'Crown' and perhaps some other young worthies joining in, and yet I have no reason to suppose that anyone did anything that might be regarded as immoral, we just had a really good evening.

Monte time was upon us again. I was to drive with Peter Garnier, Sports Editor of 'Autocar' as co-driver. Some new people were recruited from Knowldale Car Club, based in Rochdale, to make up the Mini team. Rochdale was beginning to loom large on my horizons. Peter Garnier and I were to be allowed to do a recce. Apart from the obvious advantages of learning routes and cols and the joy of continental travel, there were expenses and things like that, that were rarely all used and provided invaluable beer money for impecunious parsonical trainees. I drove to London to talk to Peter.

Monte Parsons

I had met Peter Garnier several times and we had got on well. It is very difficult to put into words how one feels about good friends. Peter was a Naval man during the war and as a West country man had some history and connections with seafaring. He was a brilliant journalist and did his job superbly, but I often wondered how someone so kind and gentle and considerate survived in life's ridiculous hurly-burly. Peter was pushed for time to do a recce but we were able to agree four or five days in early January when we could get away. Pace notes were not really yet "in" and it was more practice and training together that mattered and it was a wonderful opportunity to learn some of the important passes. I spent some hours with him at 'Autocar's' offices, journalism had always interested me. Those who were employed as journalists know that photos are an important part of the finished product and 'Autocar' was part of a group. All sorts of photographic gentlemen were sent out to photograph rallying and some were a total pain because they had "Union" ideas about hours of work, on a rally you work from before the start until after the finish if you have any desire to provide the goods. Some were not interested in providing the goods. Well there are always some idiots but why do the good guys so often lose out? There was an excellent man who took really superb rally photos and was regularly with us and worked very hard. At some point about this time he inadvisedly rolled a Rootes-owned loaned Sunbeam Rapier. He did not appear again and I enquired of Peter. He told me that rolling cars belonging to other companies was not approved and that the lad was sentenced to two years photographing for things like "Caged Birds" and "Poultry World". He did eventually appear again, and we were very glad to have him back.

When Peter and I set off in an Abingdon Mini, but not a full rally car, we made a plan to run as far south as possible and practise as many of the critical passes as possible. We crossed during the night and drove south, worked through the next night and during the next day came to the passes behind Monte. Here we worked extremely hard for many hours and I really enjoyed the driving. Some of the down hill sections particularly I could drive very fast indeed. Peter seemed to have confidence in my ability and when

I was not working too hard we talked. He was a little upset at the slaughter of a pig which we witnessed as we were held up by a farm and this led to further discussion about my stalking activities and other important issues. It was really delightful to be with someone with views worth discussing. We paused above Monte Carlo and looked down on the Med, but then turned and headed north with more work to do. After another night and day we were tiring and headed for Grenoble and a night in bed. Peter looked in the Michelin Guide for somewhere really exotic, with lots of crossed knives and forks and chef's hats, we had worked for plus of fifty hours and some sophistication seemed appropriate. He found a converted chateau and we drew in and parked. Yes, they were open but the chef was due to go out soon, we were very welcome but please would we choose our meal and having bathed and changed, come down again quite soon? Yes, of course. Trout and steak was recommended. That seemed good. Would we like to select our trout from the tank? I was selecting mine when I realised that Peter was about to faint. Eating trout was one thing but seeing it live and saying slay that one for me was another. We spent a pleasant evening but were very tired and soon retired. I felt that I could drive a good rally on what we had seen and could work very well with Peter.

At the start in Paris I met Derek Astle and Saville Woolley from Knowldale Car Club in Rochdale and they made it clear that I would be made very welcome in that part of Lancashire. If we didn't meet at the finish they said, then contact us at these addresses, and cards were exchanged. The usual pre-rally planning went on, navigators taking the brunt of this, but Peter was glad of my help, so I sat in on these sessions. Jack Sears was a team member. He was someone who I had met regularly racing but had not got to know very well until this time. His nickname ''Gentleman Jack'' was and is one hundred per cent appropriate. He is someone who has done so much for motorsport and I think had a kindly word for so many of us that I feel privileged to know him and to have been in the same team as him. Like Graham Hill, whenever I was at a circuit, Jack always seemed to make a point of coming to say ''Hello''. To the young enthusiast, especially one who was determined to do something perhaps ''different'' with his life this meant a great deal.

The night before the rally was to start we all went out for a meal and several of us had oysters. Next morning we started and worked our way east towards the Vosges Mountains and then north.

By dawn the following morning it was first very snowy and then icy and proceeding at high speed along a ''D'' road a farmer pulled out of his farmyard in front of me. I aimed to go behind him but he stopped. I tried to go in front but hit his front off side wing and ploughed into the ditch. I was injured and Peter was worse. The farmer's wife took Peter into the house to tend him while I coped

"a farmer pulled out of his farmyard in front of me ... our rally was over". One of the very rare times that I brought home a really bent motor.

with the farmer and gendarmes. Our rally was over. The second Mini got further but both crew members suffered food poisoning, put down to the oysters. Derek and Saville got close to Monte when a stone fell and came through the passenger window and struck Saville, who had to be taken to hospital for stitches. One Mini team was out. By this time Peter and I were through formalities and as the Mini was just driveable headed north to get a ferry during the night. We were in London in the early morning and Peter wanted hospital attention. I dropped him at home, took the banana shaped Mini to Abingdon, picked up Marigold and headed for Wells. I was very battered about the ribs and went to my doctor. X-rays showed that nothing was broken but there was severe bruising, so having reported into college I rested up for a while. It was nearly Easter before I could laugh or cough in comfort. So ended a Monte.

I had an interview with Marcus some days after the rally was over. My schedule was fairly busy for the forseeable future, finishing exams, moving to Rochdale and so on. We agreed that I should do the Liege with someone from Knowldale, yet to be selected, and that on the following Monte two newly-ordained clergymen should set out together in a Mini. This meant that Philip Morgan needed to do the necessary rallies to qualify for his International licence. Philip had a Mini which was rallyable by the rules of those days, so we set out. Most of our events were in Wales and we fulfilled our purpose of getting the necessary signatures and also learning to work together. We seemed to do Eppynt ranges on a very regular basis, which in later years served me in good stead, until I attempted many years later on a new road recently created by the Army, totally misread it and had an "oops, nasty". We enjoyed these outings, not winning any prizes but Philip learning the game and soon we were able to ring Marcus and say that we had cracked it and when the time came he could send in our entry, so that was to be some time ahead. While all this was going on I needed to move to Rochdale. At some point or other I rang Derek Astle to say that I was coming up to sign up with the Bishop and recce the parish. It seemed that there was a two up, two down, lavatory in backyard, Curate's house in which I was expected to live. A house of my own really suited me and I longed to see it.

Although I had been blessed with good landladies, except perhaps at Wells, I longed for independence, particularly in the culinary department. Derek said tea at his house was at 5 pm and the third Tuesday in the month was the best day, as Knowldale Committee meeting occurred at "The Birches" across the road at 7.30 pm and I would be a welcome guest. We would look at the curate's house between times. Through some chum in Liverpool my father had organised enough basic furniture, some of which Sue and I still have some thirty odd years after, but Derek found carpet and many other things that greatly assisted my arrival in Rochdale. Number one, Bay Street afforded the most fabulous views from the front of the house. The road was unmade, followed by some grass and then well tended allotments, some Common, school playing fields below and our Church up the hill to the left. Houses stretched up Halifax Road which was and is exactly what its name implies, the route to Halifax. And then lifting the eyes up to the hill, as in my father's favourite psalm "I will lift up mine eyes unto the hills", one could see Brown Wardle to the left, Blackstone Edge ahead and round towards Saddleworth Moor to the right.

But all this I was to discover later. On the third Tuesday in March 1961 I made my way to Derek's house in Rochdale for about 5 pm and we had "tater pie" for tea which may well have been put on for my benefit, but I doubt it. After tea we went down to One, Bay Street, having already obtained a key from Anthony Herbert, the Vicar, and Derek just went round with pencil and paper and said "Right, these things will be done when you arrive". This included carpeting with either new or second-hand carpet. Then we went to the committee meeting where I met Mike Sutcliffe, Don Grimshaw, Phil Crabtree and other well known rallyists of the day. After the business, during which some ale was supped, we went in Derek's ex-works Healey and by way of Healey Dell to a pub called the "Chapel House", well it wasn't named that, it had a fancy name, but that was what it was called. Here I met lots of other motoring chums and we seemed to drink even more ale. I returned to Wells next day after paying a visit to my old school friend to tell him I was about to hit Rochdale and hoped to see something of him.

I was going to be sorry to part with Wells. I had become fond of the routine, the friends and the very peaceful existence, interrupted only by rallying and a little light duck shooting, oh and heavy golf with Hugh, but all good things come to an end, so they say. Before plunging into any sort of ecclesiastical bath tub it is decreed to be necessary to go into retreat, that is silence, and talking by others directed at you. Sometimes these are valuable. Our pre-ordination retreat was at Waddon Hall near Clitheroe, a place given over largely to Girl Guides!! Being me, I arrived very early to make a reconaissance of the area. I did not book in but having established the whereabouts of various watering holes and called in at Clitheroe Parish Church for a prayer I selected a suitable house for liquid lunch and cheese.

The retreat promised to be a fairly dry affair. I don't really know how these things happen but although I had reading material with me I fell into good company at the pub of my choice and returned to Waddon later than I intended. I booked in and started up the baronial hall-type staircase with my luggage. Suddenly I was confronted with a pair of brogue shoes proceeding downwards. I politely pulled over but a powerful voice of the type I was accustomed to when hunting, demanded "Do you know who I am, young man?" and without awaiting reply continued, "I am Olive, Lady Baden Powell, World Chief Guide". Well, there really seemed to be no answer to that except sort of "Jolly good show" which somehow seemed appropriate. Anyhow, she pottered on her way to the next sausage sizzle or jamboree or whatever girl guides have, and I made my bedroom. Fierce females totally disarm me, I ought to have been able to cope with Lady Olive, but I was fairly flummoxed, and felt that a few days in silence with no one asking any ridiculous questions, like "Do you know who I am?" might be quite a good idea.

The ordination service on Trinity Sunday was really great because Manchester Cathedral was full, and a really full building dedicated to doing a certain thing creates a wealth of feeling. Mummy and Daddy were present and also a large contingent from my new parish, All Saints, Hamer, Rochdale. After service we had some lunch and then I returned to the parish to be put on view to the public at Evensong, and so started my ecclesiastical career. I left Wells with very happy memories, on a Sunday evening we theological students each had an eccesiastical slot to fill. Today in school it is called "work experience". Well the church has always been miles ahead in some fields, in fact I think it was us that really started education in this and many other countries. Some had small country parishes to go to and take evensong in the church, others of us went to a couple of wards each in Wells Infirmary to conduct prayers and a hymn or two. Some of the brethren were sufficiently skilled to use musical instruments, either imported or available on site. Mike and I had no such skill, but he could sing and I thought I could, I still do. We both have voices which can reach high notes and we were assured by "good friends" that when we were leading certain hymns we could be heard throughout the entire complex. The old boys on one ward lay in bed with their caps on but they took them off and waved them when we really hit the high notes and again when we said goodnight. Maurice was "bishop" at some small village and asked me to join him one evening and take the service and preach while he played the harmonium. We came to a point in the service where I should have led the Lord's Prayer but somehow I had forgotten this and was expecting Maurice to give me a note. Eventually he produced the necessary note and the service continued. Afterwards, I having realised my mistake, Maurice quizzed me. "Maurice", I said, "It's the third Sunday after Pontefract races, one omits the Lord's Prayer". At this time I was heavily bearded, and while driving back to Wells from some outlying parish in Marigold some unfortunate farmer crossed me. In my cassock and beard I roundly castigated him and later realised that I must have looked much more like the Devil than a theological student. Shortly after this the beard came off. We were about to start a retreat in college, and the retreat leader ate at our house before we plunged into silence. He was a man I vastly respected and after eating he took me to one side and said to me that if I wanted to get rid of my beard now was the time, because after service that Monday evening no one would be able to comment until breakfast on Friday morning. I settled down after service, hacked away and shaved and next morning when I entered the Cathedral Lady Chapel for morning prayer there were one or two gasps of breath, but by Friday it was "old hat". So now it was Rochdale and Wells had to be slotted into the memory bank, but slotted in it was, because one only banks things which are worthwhile.

Apart from my superb new pals in Knowldale someone I soon got in touch with was my racing mate of Cambridge days, Harry Ratcliffe. Harry worked for an aircraft firm locally but prepared his own car and helped one or two of the others in the evenings. He totally transformed Marigold for under twenty pounds. I got a camshaft from Abingdon and some decent carburettors and suddenly I had a superb racing van. I paid for the necessary tax and put windows in the back. There was a severe speed limit on vans in those days and the good Marigold was now a hundred mile an hour machine. I was co-opted onto the Committee of Knowldale Car Club and as my weekends were busy and therefore my help in running events was necessarily limited I started a magazine and edited that. I was also given a number of drives in various events and some cars to road test for the magazine. I very much enjoyed my parish work and got on very well indeed with my new "mad" boss, who was certainly not that. He noted that I was a drinking man and suggested that I should not make my "local" any of the pubs in the parish. This was sensible advice and petrol at that time being about one shilling and threepence a gallon, and mild beer six pence a half and no breathalyzer I found a moorland pub that suited me and made some new friends who were not into "religion" or motorsport but were a good cross section who in time were very helpful to me, not least in just introducing some reality into a religio-parochial day. Anthony Herbert, my new boss also suggested that as I was a single man, fairly well known in those days, I should beware three teenaged young ladies in the choir, and if necessary, invent a girl friend in Cheshire who I saw on days off. Frankly at that time I was too busy and not that interested, but it is delightful that now one of those three young ladies is my wife of twenty five years and the mother of our daughter. Well, not all well meaning advice works out.

So the Liege came closer and of the Knowldale people Marcus selected Don Grimshaw to drive me. I liked Don very very well but would much rather have gone with Derek Astle or Mike Sutcliffe. However, it was not my choice. Don did a recce with Tony Ambrose and what Tony told me afterwards did not encourage me. The new rally route went right through to Sofia in Bulgaria and Tony said that Don would break the car as he hit every bump or bad patch really hard. This is a difficult thing. Reading unmade roads is a real art. Don's rallying success was partly due to good navigators and plenty of prod under the right boot. Unfortunately this was not enough for a Liege. I was even less encouraged when Don told me on the way out to Liege that he was short of an exit permit and the Yugoslavs were very keen on formalities at that time. It was too late to do anything about it, and after the start my doubts were compounded when I found that he was really a total novice as far as mountain passes were concerned and once again I felt that I would have been at least as competent or even more so than my driver. I became very edgy, mentally driving as well as navigating. This was annoying because I wanted a rare three finishes in succession and I suppose I already knew that this was now highly unlikely. There were some bonuses. I persuaded Don to let me do some driving. The long trip south and east was interesting. I was used to unlit donkey carts two abreast on narrow unmade roads, but three abreast on concrete dual carriageway "autoput" (motorway) when coming up astern at 120 mph was more exciting. We had a good run through to Sofia, where at the best hotel in town we waited two hours of

Don and Rupert in the Dolomites before Yugoslavia and at this point all going well. Rupert driving. Don waves to the cameraman.

our four hour stop for an inedible meal and then set out to do battle again. Maurice Garot's good idea for leaving Sofia was a mass start for all those still in the event, and then somehow, perhaps by magic we regained our minute interval timings. Well, we didn't really, it just proved that the whole exercise was a motor race. We came out of it going well into very dusty conditions and onto some of the most vicious rallying terrain I have ever traversed. Some regular Safari competitors freely admitted that for sheer roughness, toughness, speed and endurance there was just nothing to match the Liege. Tony was right, Don hit water holes, rocks and all sorts and the poor car was taking a dreadful hammering. However we made fair progress and it was obvious that few would finish. Don and I didn't. We got to Skopje where the petrol arrangements were one old man and a hand-operated pump. Four works Healeys all requiring twenty gallons, plus lots of other rally cars were more than he could cope with, but without petrol we could not go on. The section to the coast was very rough and we charged at it, but soon after we turned north towards Dubrovnik the front suspension on my side gave up and our rally was over. When we had done a bodge-up repair job we made Dubrovnik in the early evening and booked in.

This was a town I had long wanted to see and now I had an opportunity and it did not disappoint. We ate well and walked round and I had another look in the morning before we took our bent and battered motor home. It was pleasant to motor gently up the coast and stop from time to time and then drift gently through Austria. Now we were not rallying Don was excellent company and we enjoyed ourselves. There was one snag, that missing exit permit. Had we still been in the rally I think that there would have been no problem, but the authorities had time to spare when we arrived some forty eight hours late. Don was a little aggressive which did not help, and I do hate pistol carrying chums when I have not got one. The situation was saved when Don bent to pick up some discarded document and split his pants. Communist border guards were vastly diverted by capitalist cowboy with split pants. I put twenty American cigarettes down in their view, quite a good "hard currency" and we were away.

I held discussions with Derek Astle when we returned to Knowldale territory about next years' Liege but it was not to be. After a tremendous start in international rallying I was now notching up some failures and I felt that they were not really of my making, however that's how these things go. Life was very good and with the Healey sorted, as Don had his own Healey I won the car for a few days before returning to Abingdon. Marcus Chambers was to finish as Competitions Manager and Stuart Turner to take over, however although luncheon at Abingdon was to become less liquid and more business-like Stuart honoured the Marcus arrangement for two clergymen to do the Monte together. One forgets how popular this event was. Three hundred plus entries and the majority British and through the super offices of Raymond Baxter motorsport was beginning to get some coverage. The route was to be very similar to last year which I had practised with Peter Garnier, but for publicity purposes Glasgow was the obvious start for us and not Paris.

On the way up to Glasgow the Mini seemed to be in fine fettle, and after breakfasting in the Lakes with my headmaster of school days, now retired and running a small parish, we made Glasgow for luncheon and were successfully scrutineered in the afternoon. I found myself on curiously strange territory in that most of my

"We forced east towards the Vosges". Rupert driving, Philip on the maps on the Col de Schlutz. A clerical couplet converges on Carlo.

serious rallying had been within the womb of a full works set-up and knowing our team and others makes team members. Here were a perfectly splendid crowd of privateers but very few people that I knew. It didn't matter as I got on very well with Philip and in fact some ex-BMC lads made themselves known and being from "north of the border" showed us around. Blythswood Square was the traditional starting point for British privateers and that was where we reported to with the Mini really rather early on a cold but not unpleasant January morning. We had a gentle and uneventful run over the Cheviots just encountering some ice patches and headed south to our next major control at Banbury with no problems and then headed on to Dover for the ferry. The route then took us early next morning out into Normandy and Rennes, but things were basically uneventful. Philip as a Mini owner was able to relieve me of some driving as we forced east towards the Vosges and then south to Grenoble and Chambery.

The Monte of those days was great for "goodies" handed through the car window at most unlikely times. Most were fairly useless, cheap and nasty tourist tackle but in Normandy we won two miniature bottles of Calvados and leaving them unopened went on our merry way. Even when we got into the mountains it continued to be one of the dullest rallies I have ever done, and at Chambery we were given the news that our class was amalgamated with the class above as one in our class had failed to start. This was infuriating news as we would have to drive very hard to mix it with the class

"We made Monte fairly well placed... " Rupert and Philip interviewed by the Beeb on arrival by the harbour.

The Col de Turini was traversed several times, trying hard near or at the summit of this magnificent test.

above, but loyal chums from Dunlop, Castrol and Ferodo said that they would pay bonuses on the old class basis and so we forced on. We made Monte fairly well placed, leading our original class and fifth in the one above. The mountain circuit saw us move up to third in that class after a perfectly superb outing. I felt totally at home with the Mini and with Philip and on some of the downhill sections particularly we seemed to drive very fast indeed. There was hardly any snow and even less ice. Was this a Monte or an Alpine? The Grand Prix ciruit was still used to assess final placings, a five lap dice with plenty of spectators. It occurred on the day of St. Peter and I had some church involvement with the Church of England chaplaincy. After religious duties there was no time to return to our base, the Hotel du Helder, to change, so I raced in my collar. To satisfy the publicity people Philip and I had driven from Blythswood Square to Dover in dog collars, but I had not intended to race thus attired. However I enjoyed the circuit and it seemed to amuse the spectators. I think the one really memorable thing about this Monte was the amount of publicity generated by two clergymen not only setting out, but also arriving, first in our own class, third in the class above and seventy seventh overall in a very ordinary little motorcar.

I was interviewed on radio and television before I left home, with the BBC and Stuart Hall making some film of me going about my parochial duties. In Glasgow Philip and I faced cameras and microphones and again at Banbury and Dover. The national daily papers picked up our reasonable result and the whole thing started again when we got home, so the gamble had certainly paid off for

"I enjoyed the circuit..." The Gas Works hairpin with high rise Monte behind.

the British Motor Corporation. The lads in the Competitions Department at Abingdon were well pleased and Stuart talked about next years'. The people in the parish seemed pleased and the general opinion was that some sort of clerical record or "first" had been notched up.

This was also my first real success as a driver in international rallies and it was to lead on to all sorts of things. I was already well settled in Rochdale and this was to be and still is my base and I would wish for nothing better. But I was now about to begin to build on the successes and failures of those formative years to make the rest of

"The national daily papers picked up our reasonable result ..." a 'staged' welcome home from Mummy and Daddy for the benefit of the Press.

my life, in the parish, in motorsport, and in time as a family man. For those in their teens who think that life stops at twenty one, or even eighteen, at this point for me at twenty six years old, all sorts of new avenues were opening up, and I had a good grounding to build on and take up those new opportunities.

My ordination as a Priest was scheduled for June and the Liege again in September. These events and getting down to work were my next objectives.